WRESTLING DRILLS

FOR THE MAT AND THE MIND

By Dennis A. Johnson, Ed.D

Johnson, Dennis A.
Wrestling Drills For The Mat and The Mind/ by Dennis A. Johnson, Ed. D
Copyright © 2011 by Dennis A. Johnson

Managing Editor: Diedra Harkenrider; Production Director, Text Layout and Design: Maria Bise; Cover Design: Trish Landsparger; Copyeditors: Jerry Casciani, Dennis Read

Photography:
Interior photos by Haley Conn, Danielle Hobeika, Al Elrefai, and Diedra Harkenrider; Drill Photo Models: Michael Jaskolka, Colter Johnson, Tyler Stufflebeam.
Cover photos from top to left: PSU by Ernie Lucas, Young Wrestlers by Tim Hoden, Drill photos on each side by Diedra Harkenrider, and other three photos by Danielle Hobeika.

Printed in the United States of America by Versa Press, Inc.
ISBN 978-0-9842802-7-8
Library of Congress Cataloging-in-Publication Data

MomentumMedia Sports Publishing, Inc.
31 Dutch Mill Rd.
Ithaca, NY 14850
(607) 257-6970
info@MomentumMedia.com

CONTENTS

DEDICATION

This book is dedicated to all of the women of the world who are involved with amateur wrestling; be they moms, sisters, wives, girlfriends, fans, or competitors.

Specifically, I'd like to remember the women in my life…My daughter Adrienne, my fiancé Lissy and her daughters Kristen and Haley, my sister Diedra and her daughter Erin, and my sister-in-law Melinda.

And finally this book is dedicated to my mother who recently passed…she had a heart that was so kind and nurturing but yet possessed a disposition tougher than any NCAA or Olympic wrestling champion. Ma–we miss ya!!!

PREFACE

The *Wrestling Drill Book* originally published by Human Kinetics in 1991 was endorsed by many coaches at a variety of levels including Olympic champions Bruce Baumgartner and Dan Gable. They touted the text as a useful tool for both parents of wrestlers and wrestling coaches at any level. USA Wrestling endorsed the text for beginner coaches and it was recommended reading in their coach's certification programs. The main purpose was to describe specific technique drills, warm-up drills, and wrestling-related games for the enhancement of technical wrestling development around the world, and to encourage student participation in the combative sport of wrestling.

This edition of the *Wrestling Drills: For the Mat and the Mind* remains a vital tool for teaching and coaching, whether one is a novice, seasoned, or expert wrestling coach. This edition features the addition of four new chapters including topics on mental skill drills, position drills, and situation drills. Most of the original wrestling drills are included; however many have been revised, some eliminated, and several added to meet the changing times in competitive wrestling.

The greatest addition to this book is the two new chapters dealing with mental skills drills. Ask any wrestler or coach what is the difference between two wrestlers that are equal in tactical/technical ability and the answer is usually mental toughness. Many coaches devote hours upon hours in tactical/technical physical preparation and seemingly leave mental skill development to chance due either to a lack of time or knowledge. Chapters 2 and 3 are devoted to mental skills drills designed to develop that mental toughness.

Numerous books, articles, and videos continue to be produced by coaches that illustrate the many techniques and tactics covering every phase of wrestling, from the takedown to the tilt (near fall) to the pin. The focus of this book differs from most others because the drills are designed primarily to enhance performance of the seven basic skills of wrestling (as developed by USA Wrestling in the 1980s) and to lead up to specific wrestling moves. For example, before a wrestler can effectively execute a double leg takedown, he or she must practice changing levels and penetrating.

Many of the physical drills have photos and are described with key phrases to help create mental images for wrestlers. Beginning coaches will find the wrestling games and activities especially useful for developing and maintaining interest among students. One of those activities (e.g., mat chess or sumo wrestling) just might spark the career of a future Olympian. Every coach and parent will find the mental skills drills useful in helping wrestlers develop the mental toughness needed to produce success when two wrestlers of equal tactical/technical ability meet in competition.

Coaches are continually working to improve their programs to compete successfully, whether their athletes wrestle at the novice or the international level. The many drills and games compiled in this book can be used to form a solid base for fundamental skill development and to encourage participation in any wrestling program.

FORWARD

Every wrestler wants to be a champion but not every wrestler wants to pay the price to be one. In fact, the latest research on developing athletic talent shows that it takes at least 10 years or 10,000 hours of purposeful practice to achieve expertise in any sport. Highly successful wrestling coaches know this point and it is the reason why they use a variety of drills to help wrestlers hone the many skills needed for on-the-mat success, whether that involves the physical, technical, tactical conditioning, or the mental aspects of the sport.

Great coaches at all levels of wrestling recognize that drills just don't need to be done but need to be done for a specific purpose and with a well-thought out rationale in mind. As the old adage goes, "Practice does not make perfect; planned purposeful practice does." In this book Dr. Dennis Johnson, a former wrestler, successful wrestling coach, and expert in the science of sports skills teaching and instruction, provides you with a wealth of well-thought out drills for running effective practices, whether you are a youth, high school, or elite level coach.

Yet, *Wrestling Drills: For the Mat and the Mind* is not just another good wrestling skills and drills book. Dr. Johnson understands the latest sport science research showing that champions in any sport, but especially wrestling, must develop more than just technique. They must develop their wrestling mental games. In order to accomplish this aspect of the book, Dr. Johnson enlists the help of one of America's best sport psychology specialists, Dr. Larry Lauer, to help write several new chapters. These new chapters focus on developing and drilling key mental skills wrestlers will need for success. Not only will these mental skills help your wrestlers be better prepared for wrestling success, but for life as well. There is only one sectional, state, NCAA, or Olympic champion crowned each year in each weight class, but there are thousands of young men (and now women) who learn life lessons through wrestling involvement. Just like physical skills, mental skills must be taught and practiced and will be carried through life once one's wrestling career is over. These chapters will show you how to effectively teach these mental skills.

Finally, Coach Johnson's experience as a teacher and his expert knowledge of the sports skills teaching research have taught him that while all wrestlers need to drill, train, and learn mental toughness, they are more likely to accomplish their goals if they enjoy practice. While wrestlers will always need to drill and drill hard, Coach Johnson's chapter on using a "games" approach to teaching our sport is both innovative and exciting. Kids and young men and women who participate like the act of wrestling best, so this chapter shows how you, as a coach, can be stealthy by organizing scrimmages, games, and wrestling activities to get the same benefits of drilling without having it seem like those same boring old drills. This is especially relevant for youth coaches but also gives high school and elite coaches new ideas on how to be more effective.

In summary, Dr. Dennis Johnson's *Wrestling Drills: For the Mat and the Mind*, is not your run-of-the mill wrestling drills and skills book. It builds off the latest sport science and best practice literature to show you how to help young people become all they are capable of being through wrestling. I hope you enjoy reading it as much as I did.

– Daniel Gould, Ph.D., Dept. of Kinesiology, Michigan State University

Editor's note: *Gould is a former Brockport State wrestler, chaired the Sports Science and Medicine Committee of USA Wrestling for several terms, helped developed the sport's coaching education program, was named man of the year for USA Wrestling for his sport science work and is currently a consultant to the National Wrestling Coaches Association (NWCA) developing its Leadership Academy*

ACKNOWLEDGEMENTS

I would like to thank all who have contributed to this venture:

- All of the wrestling coaches who have contributed drills, games, and/or conditioning activities
  - Specific thanks to Dean Johnson (Beaty Junior High School), Glen Baldensberger and Steve Siliano (Warren High School), and Kris Black (Eisenhower High School) who have opened their wrestling rooms to me over the years and helped me keep up with the latest in today's wrestling
  - Also to New York coaches, Aaron Zwald (Jamestown High School), and Drew Wilcox and Red Childress (Falconer High School)

- Thanks to Ken Chertew for meeting with me and allowing me to attend his Gold Medal Training Camp…he can be contacted at **www.KenChertow.com**

- Thanks to Dave Crowell of Nazareth High School for providing time to discuss his take on today's wrestling…he can be contacted for wrestling consultation at **www.DaveCrowellCoaching.com**

- Thanks to Danielle Hobeika for the use of her photos on the cover and in Chapters 2 and 3…her entire collection can be viewed at **www.amateurwrestlingphotos.com/folkstyle**

- Thanks to Diedra Harkenrider and Haley Conn for taking the drill pictures and Jerry Casciani for editing.

- Thanks to the models in the drill pictures for their time and efforts…Thanks Colter Johnson, Tyler Stufflebeam, and Michael Jaskolka.

- Thanks to the entire staff at MomentumMedia Sports Publishing

- And finally, thanks Pappy for the books you bought me and the lessons you taught me.

Chapter 1

OVERVIEW AND HOW TO USE THIS BOOK

OVERVIEW

Wrestling Drills: *FOR THE MAT AND THE MIND* includes basic wrestling drills, mental skills drills, and activities and contests covering every phase of wrestling. It should be read in its entirety and then kept on hand as a reference source. Coaches continually search for drills that will serve to improve tactics and techniques. Many of the drills in this text are useful in evaluating drill design and because they make practices more stimulating may serve to enhance overall learning and skill development.

More importantly this text provides coaches with a primer for helping wrestlers develop the mental toughness needed to be successful in wrestling. There are a number of texts on the market that discuss mental skills training in general. *Wrestling Tough* (Chapman, 2005) is one book specific to wrestling and features a number of great stories featuring some of America's toughest wrestlers. Wrestling greats such as Dan Gable, the Brands brothers, John Smith, the Banachs and the Petersons are the source for many of the inspirational stories. However, a recipe for developing the skills needed for mental toughness is not included.

Therefore, Chapter 2 of this text commences with an overview of the components involved in mental skill training; a basic generic primer on mental skills training. Topics such as goal setting, imagery, positive self-talk, relaxation/arousal control, and concentration are discussed as to the part they play in developing mental toughness. Chapter 3 follows with a "step-by-step" approach to teaching the mental game of wrestlers. Remember, a contest between two wrestlers who are equal in terms of tactical/technical abilities is usually won by the mentally tougher competitor.

As for the tactical/technical portion of the sport, lead-up drills for basic wrestling skills needed to execute takedowns, reversals, escapes, riding, and pinning are found in Chapters 4 through 9. Drills for setups including duckunder and arm drag drills are in Chapter 6. The activities in Chapter 10 will be of particular interest to the peewee and junior high coaches and physical educators because they include many games that can be played on the wrestling mat; many of these activities can also be used to promote interest in wrestling and to make practice more stimulating. Coaches attempting to keep practices from becoming boring may use the games in practice due to the fact that boredom impairs learning and skill development.

Chapter 11 includes warm-up and conditioning ideas for coaches to implement. The final two chapters of the text include live wrestling drills that can be used for the combative portion of a workout. Chapter 12 pictures an number of positions that coaches might want to start their wrestlers in for live wrestling and Chapter 13 provides a number a scenarios/situations that coaches may use to prepare wrestlers for competition.

GAMES APPROACH TO DRILLING

Since the first edition of this book in 1991 a new pedagogical approach to practice has evolved for developing a practice plan. Coaches frequently hear comments/complaints about the boredom that develops during the drill periods of practice. Wrestlers often comment, "This is so boring! "Why do we have to do it?" This often leads to lack of focus and motivation on the wrestlers part which may create a possible disconnect between the actual drilling of specific moves and how those moves actually fit into the tactical aspect of matches.

Rainer Martens in his book *Successful Coaching* (2004) suggests that traditional drilling is being ousted by this new games approach and wrestling coaches should take heed. He notes, "…the new games approach, in which the emphasis is on learning the games through game-like practice" (p.174).

Wrestling coaches might consider implementing more of the games approach to the practice setting. In the typical drill sessions, wrestlers often lose motivation in the rote repetitive drills and lose focus on the task. As a result the wrestler's transfer of technique and its application to a tactical setting (the match) is often lost.

The games approach will require extensive planning by the coach to structure match-like situations so that wrestlers learn what they need to know to do well. Coaches can do this using three methods: shaping play, focusing play, and enhancing play (Martens, 2004, p. 175-180).

Shaping play is about teaching through wrestling games. For example, a coach may use a game such as Cowboys and Indians (10.26, page 212) to emphasize a certain aspects of the match (in this case riding an opponent) and it serves to increase motivation.

Focusing play allows a coach to zero-in on key elements of the match. One technique is the "freeze replay," in which the situation is stopped and "rewound." By questioning wrestlers while replaying a move, the coach is able to help wrestlers identify the key components of proper technique. An example of this would be having the wrestlers freeze during a single leg attempt drill and asking wrestlers how they would score based on their partner's reaction.

Lastly, a coach may present challenges for wrestlers to enhance their level of technique. By restricting certain attacks (such as upper body throws), a coach can emphasize leg attacks. Another example might be requiring a certain type of set up before attacking. Many coaches already do this in terms of position and situation live wrestling (see Chapters 12 and 13).

Research has indicated that the games approach of teaching through shaping, focusing, and enhancing play helps athletes understand what the sport is about, enhances tactical/technical preparation, and elevates motivation during practice sessions. The drills and games in this text can be used to meet those goals.

TYPES OF DRILLING

There are a variety of methods used to drill, and drilling can accomplish a variety of purposes. However, coaches should use a games approach to practice whenever possible; especially during the technique, conditioning, position, and situation drilling. The various types of drills include the following:

Technique Drilling

Drilling to develop technique is executed a bit slower than combat speed, especially early in the learning process. Young wrestlers in midget programs and beginner wrestlers in middle school will drill techniques in a slowed down fashion early in their careers. Wrestlers may even participate in the whole-part method of drilling techniques. That is, they might drill certain parts of the move prior to putting the whole move together or they might actually play a game to learn a move. Obviously at the higher levels (senior high, college, international), wrestlers should drill technique at or near full combat speed.

Conditioning Drills

There is no regard to technique in this type of drill. It is designed for wrestlers to move at full combat speed and develop wrestling specific fitness. This type of drilling involves wrestling specific movement to develop strength, endurance, and aerobic and anaerobic fitness.

Shadow Drilling

This type of drilling is similar to the shadow boxing techniques utilized by fighters. It involves simply completing techniques without a partner, an Adam machine, or a throwing dummy. It can be used at any time with or without a mat (depending on techniques being practiced). This is also an excellent form of drilling if one is injured or forced to leave the wrestling room with a skin disorder (e.g., herpes, impetigo, etc.). Former Olympian Ken Chertow endorses this type of drilling at his all-star camps and clinics. Additionally, this form of drilling allows wrestlers to sharpen their ability to control their imaging, an aspect essential for the mental skills drills used to develop mental toughness.

Flow Drilling

This is the type of drilling a fan might see during the warm-ups at a college or international match. Wrestlers appear to be executing moves in a fluid motion without real concern as to opponent reaction. There is a heightened awareness as to the mental aspect during this type of drilling. The wrestler is seemingly "in the zone."

Position Drilling

This type of drilling is usually completed using live combat wrestling. That is, wrestlers are put in certain positions (e.g., single leg up, cradle locked, legs on, etc.) and are then instructed to wrestle live on the whistle. See Chapter 12 for a variety of positions that coaches may use to prepare wrestlers for competition.

Situation Drilling

This type of drill also involves live combat wrestling. A wrestler is given a situation such as being ahead by one point with 30 seconds to go in a match and in the top advantage position. This type of drilling will allow wrestlers to familiarize themselves with numerous situations and be prepared to execute an action plan. Chapter 13 contains a number of situations that a coach might use.

THE DRILL FORMAT IN THIS TEXT

Each individual wrestling drill or activity is presented and explained using the following format:

Skill Level: The drills have been designed to be used at four different levels of ability: beginner (peewee), novice (typically middle school or junior high), advanced (high school), and elite (college and beyond). The drills listed for beginner wrestlers could be used by wrestlers at the novice, advanced or elite levels. However, drills should not be used for levels lower than indicated due to physical and emotional immaturity of the participants.

Purpose: This section of each drill states what the drill is designed to accomplish in terms of wrestling skill acquisition or tactical/technical preparation. For instance, the power step penetration drill is designed to teach wrestlers a method for attacking an opponent.

Basic Skills: This section is utilized only for the neutral position drills. It will list the basic skills used in performing each drill as identified by USA Wrestling in the 1980s. In interviewing coaches, most indicated that the skills of position, motion, level change, penetration, lifting, backstep, and back arch are still integral for success in 2011 and beyond.

Prerequisite: This section briefly states the skills wrestler should be able to perform before participating in the drill.

Procedure: This is a step-by-step description of the drill, often illustrated with photographs.

Coaching Points: This section alerts coaches to key points in each drill. A key point might consist of a slight variation of the drill or include a concept wrestlers must be made aware of to understand the purpose and structure of a given situation. Sometimes the coaching point simply suggests when to use the drill.

Safety Concerns: Wrestlers should always be grouped according to weight in order to obtain maximum safety during drills and competitions. Safety concerns will be noted for any drill that has an increased risk for injury.

Summary

In summary, coaches should use this text as a resource to enhance tactical/technical preparation in their practices. Many of the drills, activities, and games will help coaches implement a "games" approach to practice planning and serve to sharpen tactics and technique while simultaneously allowing coaches to "liven up" practices during the dog days of the season. Coaches should pay special attention to Chapters 2 and 3 in order to help their charges become mentally tough. Have at it–go forth and conquer!!!

Chapter 2

Photo by Danielle Hobeika

The mentally tough wrestler is able to eliminate distractions and remain determined and focus on the task at hand.

MENTAL SKILLS TRAINING:
An Overview

Larry Lauer, Ph.D. CC-AASP
Director of Coaching Education and Development
The Institute for the Study of Youth Sports
Michigan State University

Chapter Abstract: This chapter is designed as a primer for coaches and parents who lack the basic knowledge of just what mental skills training is all about. The information in this chapter provides basic knowledge for coaches in terms of goal setting, confidence, self-talk, relaxation, imagery, and focusing. These are the basic mental skills that coaches can help their athletes develop.

INTRODUCTION

In the championship match two wrestlers are locked in combat; it's a vicious back-and-forth battle. Neither man is able to gain an edge on his opponent. Each wrestler possesses equal speed, strength, endurance, and tactical-technical preparation. Victory lies in the balance. Who will win? Likely the wrestler that has greater mental toughness will win; the one who believes in himself and is able to put aside the distractions, the tension, and the doubts and focus on a singular goal. The mentally tough wrestler is more attuned to the opponent and able to anticipate his moves and counteract them. He is able to be taken down and continue to battle. He will be willing to go for victory instead of hoping to hang on and not lose it. The wrestler that can focus on outwrestling the other guy in that moment will be victorious.

Most coaches and wrestlers would agree with the previous mental toughness claims. Ask any wrestler how much of wrestling they consider to be mental and the responses will range anywhere from 70 to 95 percent. In contrast, wrestling coaches study technique tapes for hours to keep up-to-date with the latest techniques. And, they will have their athletes spend hours on tactical/technical preparation and physical conditioning in the wrestling room. Yet when it comes to mental skills training, many coaches virtually ignore the topic. Many, in fact, resort to the age-old adage to just "be tough out there on the mat." And, others believe that "either you have it or you don't." These strategies will not bring out the best in a wrestler.

Just what is it to be mentally tough or to exhibit mental toughness? Many believe that being mentally tough means never breaking down or cracking in practice or in competition. That one never quits, regardless of the odds. That one is totally driven with the mission at hand. And the mentally tough athlete is confident and in total control, even when the chips are down.

Dr. David Yukelson, Coordinator of Sport Psychology Services at Penn State University, defines mental toughness "as having the natural or developed psychological edge that enables an athlete to generally cope better than your opponents with the many demands that are placed on you as a performer." Specifically, he suggests that they must be better than the opponent in remaining determined, focused, confident, resilient, and in control under pressure.

Thus, wrestlers that are mentally tough should have an advantage over their opponent. And, gaining this edge is under the coaches' and athletes' control. Wrestling coaches can teach their athletes a variety of strategies to enhance the possibility of their charges becoming more mentally tough. Wrestlers can be taught strategies to build confidence, a key component in mental toughness. They can be taught how to handle the pressure of big matches and remain fully focused on the mission at hand. Wrestlers can be taught skills to help eliminate worry and self-doubt. And finally, they can be taught that failure is only a temporary setback.

Dan Gable, the great Iowa State University wrestler, is often considered one of the greatest athletes and coaches in history. Remember, Gable was undefeated in college until the final match of his career when he lost in the NCAA finals. He used that as motivation to go unscored upon and win a gold medal in the 1972 Olympics. Even the great Gable was not perfect–much like Michael Jordan, who missed 9,000 shots, missed 26 game-winning shots, and lost 300 games. As Jordan said about the subject of failure, "I failed over and over, that is why I suceeded." Great athletes understand that they must risk failure in order to succeed.

Mental toughness is a necessary component of any successful wrestling program. However, many coaches are not sure where to begin and what to focus on. The remainder of this chapter provides an overview of the foundational mental toughness skills: goal setting, confidence, self-talk, relaxation, imagery, and focusing. This will give coaches the basics necessary to understand and implement the wrestling mental skill drills presented in Chapter 3.

Getting the Most out of a Wrestler's Potential:
Goal Setting, Motivation, and Mission

"Once you have wrestled, everything else is easy." Dan Gable

The growing sentiment from sport science researchers is that to become an expert of athletic technique one needs 10 years or 10,000 hours of deliberate practice. The bulk of these hours should involve the difficult task of repeating technical drills until they are mastered, doing strenuous conditioning and strength training, and rolling on the mat against an equally determined, skilled opponent. This is a lot to ask of anyone. So, understand that all wrestlers are going to struggle at times with the commitment level needed to become experts.

However, if wrestlers can develop a goal which drives them, like Gable at the Munich Olympics, they can commit for the long haul. They can stay motivated and persevere when struggling to reach their dreams. However, it takes a lot of hard work and sweat and a willingness to critically monitor progress every day.

Photo by Danielle Hobeika

Motivation is key to the hard work needed to be successful on the mat.

To catalyze the dedication of his athletes, a coach must help wrestlers become passionate about a goal; to win a championship, to be their very best, to contribute to the team's success, or be involved in something bigger than themselves. Goal setting is an essential component of any wrestling program. Yet, many coaches struggle to find the time or to gain the buy-in from their team to consistently set and strive towards goals.

We all, as do most wrestlers, informally set goals for ourselves whether it is to reach for something great or to avoid setting goals at all. The key is to bring the goal-setting process to the forefront of our consciousness and make it work for you and your athletes. Goals bridge one's current status to his dreamed potential. They provide a road map for success and beacons to focus on when times get tough.

If goals are so important why is it that many athletes don't set goals? Like many people, goal-setting can be seen as tedious or useless efforts in writing down notes. However, this will often be used as an excuse for something below the surface, they are nervous about making themselves accountable by putting their goals on paper. What do they do now if they fail? Everyone will know. Goals can create anxiety if not approached appropriately.

Therefore, the problem with goal setting is that we are often not taught to set goals that enhance our development and instead our athletes are left to their own devices to try and figure out what they should be shooting for. And, this is a game of chance that should not be played. Below is a list of reasons why goal setting can be harmful to performance if completed incorrectly.

1 **Set too many goals.** Wrestlers get excited about goal setting and then set 12 goals. The problem is that individuals really only should focus on one to maybe as many as four goals at one time. It is a mistake to split the focus in too many directions. Wrestlers will be unable to apply complete energy and attention to any one goal and the quality of effort in towards each will suffer.

2 **Set only outcome goals.** Outcome goals are based on winning and being better than someone else. These goals can be highly motivating short term. However, we don't have control over these goals, and with a reliance on outcomes to feel successful what keeps an athlete motivated if his or her team is losing, or if he or she is struggling on the mat?

3 **Set the bar too low.** When goals are set too low we achieve them easily and then fail to set another goal that challenges us to continue to improve. Setting goals too low minimizes development. A prime example is the wrestler that has the primary goal of wrestling varsity in his weight class, reaches this goal, and the rests on his laurels in practice because he has not envisioned himself beyond his current situation.

4 **Set the bar way too high.** When goals are too difficult frustration grows and the wrestler is more likely to stop going after them. Many teams suffer from having very challenging season-end goals that fail to keep athletes motivated in the "dog days" when they are tired, injured, or just plain not feeling good about themselves as wrestlers. Difficult goals should be broken down into shorter, more attainable goals that lead to the difficult goal. This allows for constant feedback and a feeling of progress towards the ultimate goal as athletes feel they are improving.

5 **Give up too quickly.** Many athletes write down a goal and then when they don't reach it in the next practice they give up on it. They must stick to their goals. However, many of us are stubborn and anything short of reaching the goal is total failure. This is an attitude which needs to be adjusted! Wrestlers should think about why they did not reach the goal and then come up with an adjusted goal, a new way of reaching the goal, or recommitting to the already established plan.

6 **Have no goal achievement strategies.** Without a plan how does an athlete know what course is needed to achieve the goal? It is amazing how many times athletes set goals without a clear plan for reaching them. Coaches must facilitate the process of athletes not only setting goals, but coming up with effective ways to work towards them. This, of course, is vital when wrestlers are working out without coaches. What kinds of practices will they have without having a clear goal-focus?

Why should wrestlers set goals if there are many ways that it can be harmful to their motivation and performance? Because the benefits far outweigh the risks, and, wrestlers must learn that being evaluated and having goals is not a bad thing. It will keep them focused and motivated. It will direct their attention on most important areas to improve, enhance their coach's opinion of their dedication and preparation, and help them stay on course, learn from losing, and fuel efforts to persevere instead of giving up. Finally, attaining goals helps to build confidence. The world outside of sport forces us to set goals so it's best to learn effective goal setting in wrestling so it can be used in school, business, and relationships.

Goals can reinforce confidence from wins and lessons from losing.

Photo by Danielle Hobeika

Goals as a Window to Long Term Motivation for Training and Competition

We all have tendencies in how we set goals. It depends on our predominant view of success. What does success mean to you? Whether it's winning, developing athletes, or teaching life skills whatever we initially direct our sights on is usually our primary focus on how we view success. The key is to have wrestlers focus on three different types of goals so that they set themselves up for success in competition.

1 **Outcome Goals.** Focus is on comparing one's self with an outside standard such as another competitor, rankings, championships, trophies, praise from coaches, parents or teammates, or accolades in the media.

2 **Performance Goals.** The standard is comparing the performance against one's own previous performances. Thus, goals such as scoring the first takedown of the match or getting to one's feet using a standup from the bottom referee's position help to keep the wrestler focused on his own performance and getting better. Goal attainment is not contingent on factors outside personal control. Therefore, the likelihood of achieving success and staying motivated is higher. When athletes feel they are making progress they will persevere even if not reaching their ultimate outcome goal yet.

3 **Process Goals.** These are the "how-to" goals or how to perform and reach the desired outcome. For example, "I will clear my arm on all standup attempts" or "I will keep my head up on my penetration shots." Process goals are essential for the competitive wrestler because they direct the focus to the "here and now" of competition and to the tactics and techniques needed to be successful. Facilitating wrestler focus on process goals is crucial for focusing on small incremental gains and a focus on getting better every day, especially as it relates to learning from losing.

The fundamental concern with outcome goals is that they can decrease intrinsic motivation to compete. Thus, an outcome goal of paying someone for pins is excellent for fueling short term motivation, but in the long run does not motivate wrestlers to continue competing. This is due first to the fact that outcome goals are not under our direct control. The other wrestler could be better on that day despite an excellent performance. If the athlete is only outcome focused they will not perceive the good things that were accomplished. In this way they will then only take the bad from the match, not see what they did well, and thus potentially lower their self confidence and motivation.

Using the earlier example of paying for pins will illustrate another issue with outcome goal focus. Outcome goals are extrinsically rewarding. The external reward of money for pins can become the main reason why the athlete wrestles (from an earlier stage where it would have been about enjoyment, getting better, being on a team, etc.). This shift is damaging when payment for pins is removed. Now the athlete is less motivated to continue to compete because the motive previously switched from doing it because they wanted to succeed or for the love of wrestling to doing it for the money. A sole focus on outcome goals also can be damaging because the athlete can perceive external forces such as parental support as contingent on something they don't totally control–winning. This is why wrestlers should never solely wrestle for their parents. Their motivation will suffer and they may even resent their parents for being the reason they wrestled.

The point here is to not downgrade outcome goals for the sake of performance and process goals. Instead, wrestlers should set all three kinds of goals. Naturally many wrestlers will tend to focus on the outcome goals. Thus, as the coach or parent, you will need to challenge them to set performance and process goals. The athlete that commits to all three types of goals has the pride and desire to win and be recognized for accomplishments, while at the same time understanding that it is important to focus on the daily habits of improvement that lead to the outcome goals. Like Dan Gable, they will be driven to be better than their opponents, but be able to focus on the process and thus persevere despite setbacks. At the same time they will be able to reduce competitive anxiety (e.g., less likely to have doubts relative to uncontrolled standards of success).

In summary, taking into account individual differences, wrestlers should:

- *Have all three types* of goals in their arsenal

- *Focus on performance* and process goals when anxious, when learning from losing, and focusing on techniques and tactics

- *Focus on outcome* goals when flat, fatigued, lazy, or in strenuous training where they need a boost

Earlier it was mentioned how goals are often set in a harmful way. To overcome this it is recommended that wrestlers set SMART Goals.

That is:

1 **Specific:** explains exactly what will the wrestler do (I will focus on scoring takedowns using an arm drag setup)

2 **Measurable**: provides a number, quantity, percentage, a numerical marker of knowing if the goal has been met (I will score three takedowns on two different opponents during scrimmage.)

3 **Action Positive**: focuses on what "I will do" versus "I won't" or "Don't" (I will be aggressive and score using an arm drag during the scrimmage session.)

4 **Realistic**: is within the person's reach and yet challenging (If I am a varsity wrestler, I must be able to score on other varsity wrestlers and not just on the JVs.)

5 **Time (frame)**: when will the goal be achieved (In this case during one practice session.)

Applying the SMART principles to goals allows athletes to positively motivate themselves, set achievable goals while pushing their limits, and makes it easier to monitor success. Thus, wrestlers that set these goals will more likely recognize their success on all three kinds of goals because they will not only think about what success would be, but also know how to measure it. And the more often goals are achieved, the more the confidence grows.

In the next chapter we will begin setting goals based on an evaluation of current wrestling performance. We will identify key areas that are strong and not so strong and make those the focus. When finished doing the exercises, athletes should feel they have a better understanding of what drives them, and how they want to reach their goals.

Believing in Your Mission: *Confidence*

While goal setting is crucial to the competitive wrestler, confidence may be the most important attribute needed to succeed. This book's author Dennis Johnson recalls a story about himself as an eighth grader asking a varsity wrestler a very important question. He asked this wrestler what he thought about in regard to wrestling and why was he so good. His response was that he just watched himself in his mind winning matches…all the time. From that point on Johnson indicated he visualized himself beating the best in the state while he was on a tractor mowing hay or at night before going to sleep. These constant positive visuals led to his confidence. It was not something he was born with but was instead created out of a discipline to use imagery and positive affirmations. He created a vision and believed in it.

Confidence is believing in your mission.

Photos by Danielle Hobeika

11

As a practicing sport psychology consultant the majority of athletes that meet with me talk about a lack of confidence. While confidence may not be the original reason they were struggling, it most certainly becomes the most significant reason in their perception.

Self-confidence can be defined as a belief in one's abilities to successfully perform a task or desired behavior. The self-belief wrestlers have to perform on a stage, one-on-one, in front of others is often the deciding factor between winning and losing. He who believes in himself, trusts in his training, his coaches, his conditioning, and his tactical-technical preparation will compete in the moment and not second-guess or doubt as he performs.

Sources of Confidence

Where does self-confidence come from? Athletes can gain a sense of confidence from many sources. First and foremost are previous successes. If a wrestler has a history of getting out of tough situations, coming from behind, and getting the job done, they are more likely to have resilient self-confidence in these situations. As I am sure your intimately aware, previous success is the most powerful form of self-confidence. But what if history is not on your side?

Jon Condo, a long snapper for the Oakland Raiders, was a Pennsylvania state wrestling champion in the 275-pound class despite being less than 215 pounds. Dave Caslow, writer for *Pennsylvania Wrestling Newsmagazine* (April 2010) and former Head Wrestling Coach at Philipsburg-Osceola High School, details the story of how Condo bounced back from losing a match to state rival Tim Taylor.

> The story is an illustration of two talented and mentally tough athletes who created one of the most exciting experiences of my entire coaching career. During his senior season, Jon moved up to 275-pound class (there was no 215-pound class) but could not get his weight above 211 to 215 because he worked so hard. Jon Condo went undefeated until the Northwest Regional semi-finals, when he lost by a 7-4 score to three-time PIAA state place winner Tim Taylor from rival Clearfield High School. Condo had dramatically defeated the much bigger Taylor in a regular season dual meet to hand the state's top ranked wrestler his only loss of the year. When Taylor avenged that loss in the Northwest Regional Tournament, he celebrated by blowing kisses to the raucous Philipsburg-Osceola fans. The noisy reaction by the Philipsburg-Osceola fans nearly blew the roof off the Clarion University gymnasium. Taylor followed by winning the regional championship and Condo wrestled his way back to place third, the stage was set for the third Condo/Taylor match at the PIAA State Championships the following week.
>
> One of the local newspapers printed a large photo of Tim Taylor blowing kisses toward the rowdy Philipsburg-Osceola fans while celebrating his regional win. Someone made numerous copies of the photo and posted them in the halls at Philipsburg-Osceola High School. The hype from fellow students, fans and media was extreme! Along with mental toughness, focus, poise and strategy would be necessary for Jon's mission at the PIAA State Championships. Condo and Taylor both won their first two matches at the state tournament to set up their third match in the semi-finals. Taylor had scored four takedowns over Condo in their first two matches; however, he failed to score any in their state semi-final bout. Condo scored a takedown toward the end of the first period and won 3-2. He went on to win in the finals and finish the season with a 36-1 record. The four wrestlers that Condo defeated in the 2000 PIAA State Tournament eventually won a total of 10 PIAA state medals between them.

Condo's resiliency is definitely an inspiration for all wrestlers that each match is a new one. If you work hard and believe, you can bounce back!

If a wrestler does not have previous success on his side, say for instance he has lost three times to an opponent prior to their fourth match-up; they must rely on other sources to boost their confidence. Vicarious experience can be an excellent source of self-confidence. If the wrestler can watch video of another wrestler beating their opponent, it can boost their confidence to do the same. Or, they can watch NCAA matches and gain confidence from watching some of the best wrestlers in the world compete.

A third source of confidence is from imagined experience. This, of course, pertains to imagery and visualization. If your wrestler can imagine/visualize himself beating this opponent as Dr. Johnson did as a young wrestler, or at least use imagery to see himself performing well, he will gain a boost in confidence.

Optimal physical and mental preparation is a critical fourth source of confidence. Having an excellent week of practice often lifts the confidence of wrestlers. Wrestlers that are goal-focused, healthy, and feel ready will enter the competition with a greater sense of confidence. The fifth source of confidence is also a component of preparation; physical conditioning. Wrestlers that know they can battle for the entirety of the match, and believe they are more fit than their opponent will have more confidence.

Finally, two other sources of confidence are thinking confidently and verbal persuasion. When athletes use positive self-talk they will begin to be more confident. This includes how they assess their own physiological states (e.g., are the butterflies interpreted in a positive or negative manner?) and emotional states (e.g., when I am angry I perform well). Additionally, when their support sources encourage them, and even persuade that they are capable of the task of beating an opponent, then the wrestler should have a boost in confidence–if the source is reliable and the message is realistic. For instance, Condo may have used the picture of Taylor blowing kisses to the crowd to boost his confidence by thinking he was overconfident and thus vulnerable.

What Wrestlers Attribute Performance to Influences Confidence

How wrestlers explain success and failure has a major influence on their confidence. After an excellent performance if a wrestler attributes his performance to stable (it will be repeated), controllable, and internal factors then he will be confident in his chances of further success. If the athlete attributes failure to stable, uncontrollable factors then he will likely have a decrease in confidence. The message here is that wrestlers should not look at failure as a permanent evaluation of their abilities, nor should they become overconfident because of previous successes. They should look at each situation as an opportunity to compete and not assume victory or defeat. As a coach or parent, if you have a defeated wrestler help him attribute performance to controllable factors like effort, strategy–give him a sense of hope. And, for the overconfident athlete who does not perform to their capabilities but wins anyway, attributions about the subpar performance could be made to unstable factors (e.g., luck, bad performance by opponent), internal factors (e.g., lack of preparation), and controllable factors (e.g., working harder in practice).

Self-Limiting Beliefs and Harmful Patterns of Thinking

Many athletes believe confidence should be a quick fix. "Give me a mental trick or a magic pill, and I'll be better than ever." Sorry, it does not work that way! Confidence is a deep-down belief in one's capabilities to rise to the occasion; to be able to complete a task successfully. If a wrestler attempts to be positive on the mat, but throughout the practice week visualizes being pinned, losing, or not performing, the likelihood he can trust and focus on the task is not good. That is why it is important for wrestlers to know themselves and take a close look at their self-limiting beliefs. These beliefs are like ceilings. These are the reminders from the dark recesses of the brain saying "you are not good enough," "you cannot do this," "it will not happen," "you cannot make it." Confident athletes have fewer of these self-limiting beliefs or at least have raised the ceiling on how good they can be high enough that it is not an issue at the current level of performance. An example of having a high ceiling is when the author recalled a time when he was forced to go up a weight class and was about to face a state runner-up. The entire team, including coaches, were sure he would get pinned. However, Johnson had one great move and felt deep down that if he got his move, he had a chance to pin the state place winner and win the match. Although he didn't win, he didn't get pinned and went on to a successful season.

These self-limiting beliefs or patterns of harmful thinking do not allow wrestlers to totally believe in their abilities.

Some of the more common harmful patterns of thinking include:

- **Pessimism**: "glass half empty," always seeing the negative side of things. "I never perform well when my match doesn't start on time."
- **Negative Perfectionism**: everything must go right, and if doesn't it is horrible and I am a failure. A conversation you often hear with perfectionist goes like this. The coach: "Hey, Johnny what do you think about your performance?" Johnny: "Coach, I was not good today. Totally awful." Coach: "Johnny you lost a close match to the #1 guy in the state. And, you kept good motion on your feet and you had several perfect level changes that led to good penetration just like we talk about in practice!" Johnny: "Yeah, but I still lost. I guess I'll never be good enough."
- **Outcome Only**: focus only on winning or being better may lead to stress, lack of preparation, effort, and persistence. "As long as I win it doesn't matter what happens."
- **Self-Handicapping**: "this ought to be easy" or "there is no way I can beat this guy." Predicting one's chances of success before the competition affects the kind of preparation and focus the wrestler brings to the mat.
- **Catastrophizing**: exaggerating mistakes/losses reduces confidence; "I cannot show my face at school again after losing this match. My parents think I'm horrible."

- **Poor me**: "coach has it in for me," the athlete is looking for pity and not taking responsibility.
- **Entitlement**: a belief that you deserve something because of who you are versus your effort or performance. "I deserve this. I shouldn't have to work anymore to get it. It's my position."
- **Unrealistic**: the thought process does not lead to effective focus, "we don't need to do the off-season conditioning. We can catch up once we get into camp."
- **Past and Future Thinking**: the focus is no longer on the moment. "I can't believe I did that" and "If I can only just hang on here."

When these patterns of thinking become habitual responses then it will be a difficult chore to boost confidence. Often, until athletes challenge these types of thinking for being irrational or just plain damaging, they will struggle to maintain high levels of confidence. They are their own worst enemy.

Disciplined Self-Talk

The constant stream of things going on in our head, the messages we send to ourselves, is called self-talk. When uncontrolled, as mentioned previously, it can damage a wrestler's confidence. When a wrestler takes control and begins to use 2P thinking (positive and productive) he now can focus on the reality of the situation and begin to boost his own confidence.

Our self-talk is tied into all of our mental toughness attributes and skills. How an athlete perceives goal setting will make all the difference if he will buy-in and stay focused. Self-talk also directs our focus. When our self-talk is on something irrelevant or negative then that is where the athlete is consciously, not on performing. And, of course, self-talk has a major role in determining our level of confidence.

When self-talk is unmanaged it has a tendency to focus on judging performances while they are happening. The brain wants to assess its chances of winning and losing (thus why it is important to set process goals to attempt to refocus the mind in the moment). The mentally tough performer is capable of reframing harmful patterns of thinking and refocuses back on what matters most in competition.

The purpose of this chapter is not to present the solutions, only to overview confidence and other mental skills. To help the wrestler stay confident, or regain it, Chapter 3 will present several important confidence-boosting skills including the ability to reframe thinking, thought stopping, refocusing, dealing with mistakes and losing, and 2P thinking as a lifestyle–not a trick.

Arousal and Stress Management

Wrestling is an intense, combative sport. Rolling on the mat is not for the faint of heart. Wrestling, then, by its nature, can create a great deal of anxiety and stress. You know that the guy across from you wants nothing more than to pummel and pin you. We have all seen teams and/or individual wrestlers that are about to compete in a "big" match then due to the stress of the situation go out, appear physically exhausted and flame-out with a loss. On the other hand we have also seen wrestlers who were very loose and relaxed go out and pummel much better wrestlers because of their approach to the situation. Competitors that are able to manage these feelings and fears are most likely to be successful.

What is Arousal?

Photo by Danielle Hobeika

Some wrestlers need to be calm and some excited to perform at their best.

The mentally tough wrestler will have the ability to reach an optimal level of arousal while at the same time minimizing their stress. What is arousal? Authors Dr. Dan Gould and Dr. Bob Weinberg in their book *Foundations of Sport and Exercise Psychology* (Weinberg & Gould, 2011) consider arousal to be the physiological and psychological activation of a person that falls on a continuum from low intensity (deep sleep) to high intensity (extreme excitement). In laymen's terms, arousal is the energy we feel that comes from both physical and psychological processes.

Arousal, of course, is critical to successful performances in wrestling. Wrestlers must be aroused enough to compete at the speed, strength, agility, and alertness needed to execute their moves. At the same time, they can have too much energy and be unable to focus their attention on relevant cues like their opponent relaxing after a failed shot as they come back to the neutral position. Or they have way too much "nervous energy," and burn their energy too early in the competition.

As mentioned earlier, there is an optimal level of arousal needed for success. This optimal level on the arousal continuum, however, is different for each wrestler. Some wrestlers want to be very intense and activated. They are jumping up and down as they are about to step on the mat. Others want to be calmer and are exhibiting almost a peaceful state as they begin the match. I like to think of it as a state of intensity without tension.

Randy Hinderliter, USA Wrestling Gold Certified Coach and Coaches Education and Certification Director from Kansas, shares this true story at his clinics regarding two brothers and their match preparation.

"Years ago I knew this wrestler who was pretty solid. Thirty minutes before his bout, in his pre-match preparation, he would be running sprints. I don't mean just three or four … I mean 15 or 20 down the longest hallway he could find. Twenty minutes pre-match, he would start beating himself up … he would start slapping himself, his face, his arms, his legs … he would slap himself! This was a red-headed, fair skinned wrestler so when he slapped himself and he would leave red welts all over his body! Ten minutes before the bout, he would put on his headphones and starting bouncing! But when it came "go time" you had better have yours strapped on because his was … (he was) a three-time State Champ with 125 takedowns his senior year. This was a kid that beginning his 7th grade year, did 100 fingertip pushups every night before he went to bed. He won his State finals as a senior in 47 seconds!

A few years later, I knew his brother. I have asked their parents several times, and they vow that they are full genetic brothers! Thirty minutes before an upcoming match, the brother would be setting in the bleachers doing his calculus homework. Twenty minutes prior, he would put his calculus up and get out his physics homework. Ten minutes before, he would put all the books away, dig out his Game Boy and start playing Tetris. About three minutes before, he would saunter out of the bleachers, do a few ballerina stretches and step to the line. You better have yours strapped on because his was (i.e., headgear)… 257 takedowns his senior year … that led to a State Championship.

I ask, which brother was correct in their preparation? The answer … both! However, if you had asked the older brother to prepare like the younger … or vice versa … neither would have had the success they had (R. Hinderliter, personal communication; July 13, 2010).

The lesson of this story and the key is for each wrestler to determine what level of arousal he needs to succeed. In Chapter 3 the methods for determining this will be presented.

The Stress Impact

So, we have defined arousal but what then is stress? Stress is closely linked to our arousal levels and modulates it up and down the continuum. Stress can be viewed as a cognitive appraisal that an imbalance exists between the physical and psychological demands placed on a person, and their perception of their ability to respond to those demands. It exists in situations where not meeting the demand has important negative consequences. For wrestlers, every meet has important consequences, thus the potential for stress is inherent to the sport.

The easiest way to conceptualize stress is through the following model:

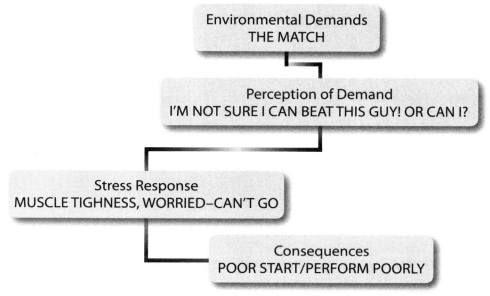

Adapted from Weinberg & Gould, 2011, p.82

An example of the stress process would be the demands a wrestler experiences prior to the conference meet. He is dealing with the most important meet of the year to-date, concerned about the partisan crowd of the host team, dealing with borderline grades, and lofty expectations from himself and others around him that he cannot lose. Wow, those are some demands, but not uncommon.

The next step is the tipping point, does the wrestler appraise the situation as something he can cope with or is it beyond his perceived coping ability? If he feels he can cope with the situation, — "What is new? Been here and done that before, — then he will experience little stress. However, if the wrestler has doubts that he can succeed with all of these demands then a more stressful response occurs.

What is the stress response? The stress response is an increase in arousal level (besides other physiological responses) accompanied by doubts and worries. Thus, it is an uncomfortable feeling that can decrease the confidence and focus of an athlete.

In the last stage of the stress process, the wrestler experiences the consequences. If little stress is experienced the wrestler will be able to perform as normal. On the other hand, if experiencing much stress the wrestler will feel tense, uncomfortable and "nervy," and suffer performance decrements in many cases.

It is important to understand this stress process because knowing it allows coaches, parents, and athletes to intervene in effective ways. For instance, using our previous example, the wrestler could have reduced his stress by doing better in the classroom; something he controls. In contrast, he cannot affect the partisan crowd so he is better off to reframe his appraisal of the crowd noise (e.g., "It gets me pumped when fans are booing") or not concern himself with it.

Effects of Stress Physically, Emotionally, Psychologically

Photo by Danielle Hobeika

The mentally tough wrestler can block out the crowd and relax under pressure.

From reviewing the stress process model it becomes clear that wrestlers are constantly being faced with demands. Mentally tough wrestlers will have strong coping skills and an understanding of themselves and when to enact particularly useful skills. A simple way to think about reducing the stress experienced by wrestlers is to look at the sources of stress and determine what sources are under the person's control and thus changeable. Then, efforts should be made to effectively manage the most significant stress sources that can be changed and also enhance the athlete's ability to respond in emotionally positive ways. Chapter 3 will illustrate a menu of stress busting strategies that will either change the demands or help the athlete cope with them.

Relaxation under Pressure

Imagine going into Iowa or Iowa State as an opponent and attempting to perform in those raucous conditions. By just being in those gyms with their traditions and the passion for wrestling, the level of intensity and a wrestler's arousal is going to be elevated. How well the wrestler performs in this environment may hinge on their ability to relax and focus on the job at hand.

If arousal and stress play such significant roles in the success and failure of wrestlers then they must develop skills to manage them. The mentally tough wrestler has the capability to relax under pressure thus reducing feelings of nerves, tension, doubts, and worries. They are able to focus on the task, remain confident even after setbacks, and allow their overlearned skills to be executed almost as if on automatic pilot. Often this is the mental skill that separates the champion from the underachiever.

What is Relaxation?

Relaxation is by its nature a positive sensation. It is a state where an athlete is physically and mentally comfortable, at a low level of tension and stress, and not experiencing stress-producing thoughts. In summary, it is a feeling of peacefulness. It is often used to reduce the high arousal wrestlers experience prior to competition.

Why would a wrestler want to feel peaceful, comfortable, and generally relaxed? The benefits are many ranging from improved health and happiness to reduced stress. Competitively speaking, relaxation allows the athlete to slow down and calm down in a stressful situation. By doing so, the athlete is able to quiet their mind of distractions, focus on the most important cues, react to the surrounding environment versus being stuck in their own head and overthinking the performance, and hopefully get into flow.

Relaxation is a foundational skill for the mentally tough wrestler, and will facilitate the use of other mental skills such as imagery, centering, and focusing. Every athlete should have mastered several ways of relaxing prior to the peak part of the season because as the saying goes "you don't need it until you need it." At some point in their careers even the loosest, most relaxed wrestlers can benefit from relaxation. No one is immune to stress.

How Does Relaxation Work?

Relaxation is an effective method for 2P (Positive and Productive) Thinking reducing stress and tension because it leads to physical and mental responses. From a physiological perspective, the relaxation response decreases heart rate, slows and makes breathing regular, decreases tension in muscles, and creates overall calmness. Mentally, the athlete is better able to shift their focus from irrelevant or harmful thoughts and environmental cues to performance-relevant cues and 2P Thinking. Acquiring a state of "relaxed intensity" allows the athlete to think rationally about problems and situations, make better decisions with a focus on options and consequences, and eliminate fear of failure by focusing on the physical sensation of the muscles relaxing and the rib cage moving and/or a mental mantra (such as counting the length of the inhale and exhale cycles).

Forms of Relaxation

When coaches and sport psychologists present the concept of relaxation to athletes they often have reactions that relaxation is hypnosis and meditation, and not relevant. While those are accepted forms of relaxation, there are other forms of relaxation that are more readily accepted by male combat sport athletes. Relaxation can be doing meditation and visualization, but it can also take more active forms like taking a walk, listening to music, doing yoga or tai chi. In Chapter 3 we recommend several popular relaxation strategies that transfer well to practice and match environments. These include deep or controlled breathing, progressive muscle relaxation, and centering.

Relaxation as a Life Skill

Many times athletes and coaches consider mental toughness and mental skills training as special topic sessions that can be use as quick-fixes or "tricks." On the contrary, relaxation (as well as the other mental skills presented in this chapter) should be considered a skill to be trained over a career and a part of a mentally tough wrestler's lifestyle. How often have you seen wrestlers carry the distractions and stress from the rest of the day into the locker room and on the mat? How have they performed? Probably not well. Wrestlers that can make several forms of relaxation a part of their life, such as going for walks and clearing their mind of distractions, listening to music, and doing deep breathing prior to going to bed, will be able to manage their stress at a lower level. This has very important health consequences but also will enable the wrestler to focus more in practice and matches, and enjoy their sport more. Therefore, do not treat relaxation as something to be used only when an athlete is "stressing out." Instead, make it a part of a wrestler's daily habits and he will reap the benefits of lower stress over time that will enable him to manage high stress situations better.

In Chapter 3 you will learn the details of how to do high-quality relaxation, several different types of relaxation techniques, how to transfer for them to pre-match and match situations, and, finally, to make this skill a component of a recovery plan.

Using Imagery to Learn, Prepare, and Compete

Imagery is likely the most recognized technique when people think of sport psychology, and also probably the most poorly or misused technique. What do you think of when someone mentions imagery? Daydreaming? Mystical and not practical? How was it presented to you and how has that influenced your belief in its effectiveness? My hope is that you do not have a less than positive impression of imagery, but these impressions are common because of lackluster experiences with the technique. Therefore, the goal of this section is to dispel any myths about this important mental skill and demonstrate how imagery is a powerful tool that can be used in many ways and in many different situations.

Most wrestlers use some form of imagery; that is they often watch themselves in their own mind executing technique or competing in matches. Dan Gable, in his book *Coaching Wrestling Successfully*, (Gable, 1999) emphasizes the use of positive imagery as a way to simulate live drilling and as a great source of motivation. Imagery, in fact, has many applications. It can be used as a tool to rehearse technique to prepare for a drill or as reflection to review task execution and give one's self feedback on the performance. Imagery also is often used to prepare for competition. Competitors will see the surroundings they will perform in, recreate the feelings and thoughts they will be experiencing, and imagine their game plan and successful execution. It gives the athlete a "been there, done that" feeling when actually entering the situation. Imagery can also be used to review matches and learn from them. Furthermore, imagery is useful in terms of enhancing concentration, confidence, motivation, controlling emotions, and even dealing with pain, injury and performance barriers. Finally, imagery can be used to rehearse routines and the use of mental skills in competition.

What is imagery? It is a re-creation of an experience, or the piecing together of memory pieces to form meaningful images in the mind. While imagery is conducted separate from reality, when done well imagery simulates or closely reflects previously lived experiences as well as experiences coming in the future.

Enough of the scientific jargon; imagery is like daydreaming but with intention. It is done with the purpose of recreating an experience to boost confidence, readiness, motivation, and focus. Imagery is not voodoo; there are a number of studies to show that athletes prefer imagery as a performance enhancement tool.

Author and sport psychologist Dr. Terry Orlick probably explains the importance of imagery better than anyone. "In sport, mental imagery is used primarily to help you get the best out of yourself in training and competition. The developing athletes who make the fastest progress and those who ultimately become their best make extensive use of mental imagery. They use it daily as a means of directing what will happen in training, and as a way of pre-experiencing their best competition performances" (Orlick, 1990 p. 66).

Imagery is more than Visuals

You have probably heard of the term visualization. Imagery differs from visualization because it accounts for all of the senses. Thus, it goes beyond the visual sensory system to include kinesthetic (or movement sensations such as body position, joints, leverage, etc.), auditory (hearing the crowd buzzing and your opponent struggling to get free), tactile sense (the feel of grabbing your opponent in the right place for a successful move), and olfactory sense (smell of the wrestling room). Including all of the senses is important because the athlete wants to create the closest representation to reality as possible. It makes the imagery experience more believable and thus more effective.

Therefore, the key for facilitating effective use of imagery is to use all of the senses. The imagery experience will mirror reality and conjure the emotions and thoughts that accompany the experience. For example, if the athlete wants to have a better performance the second time around at a particularly loud and oppositional gym he should relive the experience via imagery, remember those thoughts and feelings that helped to create the poor performance, and then began to replace them with the thoughts, feelings, and behaviors he wants to occur in his second opportunity.

Imagery Perspective

Imagery success does not rest only on the use of the senses. Its effectiveness is influenced by many factors including the perspective used by the athlete. An internal perspective is executing imagery from your own vantage point—from one's own eyes. The performance occurs from a first person view as it would in reality. For example, a wrestler would see his opponent, feel his hands making contact, but would not see his entire body from the outside perspective.

The external perspective, then, is the third person perspective. It is seeing yourself as if you were in the stands or watching the performance on television. Using this perspective then allows the athlete to view his or her whole body in action from a distance.

Which perspective is better? The author noted that he used an internal perspective when developing technique and a movie camera approach when preparing for competition. However, the verdict is still out on this question. What is more important is that both perspectives are used in a way to create vivid, controllable images.

Vividness and Controllability of Imagery

Photo by Danielle Hobeika

Concentration and focus are important. In this case is getting the pin, not getting pinned, or just having fun wrestling what's important?

Again, the use of all senses is critical to effective imagery. The image experience should create a real simulation. Thus, the vividness of the imagery is important. In doing imagery, wrestlers should pay close attention to the details of their environment such as the facility, surface, and equipment. These details can then be recalled accurately and in living color. At the same time, the athlete wants to also gain a vivid sensation of the emotions experienced as well as the thoughts that are occurring. Further, self-talk strategies can be practiced by using imagery. In Chapter 3, a vividness script is included so wrestlers have a template for creating vivid images.

While the vividness or the clarity of the details is important, maybe even more important is control of the images. Can the athlete make the imagery do what he or she is asking it to do? For example, a wrestler is attempting to use imagery to rehearse a single leg takedown with a head tap setup and a pull-through finish. Vividness will be important for the wrestler to see it, feel it, etc., but also to seeing it accurately, at the right speed, with successful performance of the move. In fact, some would argue that negativity is often imagined experiences that are not being controlled. Imagining the self losing, performing poorly, and responding in ineffective ways disrupts the athlete's focus, decreases confidence, and does not create a feeling of readiness. Therefore, wrestlers using imagery must practice this technique and master it. Being able to do a positive imagery session (i.e., imagining success against an opponent that seems unbeatable) reveals a great amount of self-belief as well as generates belief. In Chapter 3 a controllability script is provided to assist in the process of gaining control over imagery.

Developing Optimal Concentration:
Focusing under Adversity and Pressure

How many times have you told yourself, an athlete, or a co-worker to focus? It is likely too many to count for sure; we use the term focus all the time to describe the need to put our attention into one aspect of our lives intently.

Focus is a critical aspect of wrestling performance. Concentrating on the task at hand makes all the difference in competition. How often have athletes said "I lost my focus," "I wasn't focused," or "I had a hard time concentrating," after a poor performance? Again, I am sure it is too many to count.

For the wrestler, concentration is a necessity to survive against an opponent that is ready to take them to the mat. One distraction at the wrong time can be the difference between scoring a takedown and being taken down.

What is Concentration?

Concentration is simply paying attention to what one needs to pay attention to. It is focusing mental effort on external and internal events and involves four distinct kinds of focusing:

1. **Selective attention**: focusing on the most relevant cues in the moment that will lead to success.

2. **Maintaining focus over the time needed to perform**: over the course of a match, pre-match, during a tournament.

3. **Situational awareness**: understanding time, place, score and being able to make decisions accurately based on this information.

4. **Shifting focus as needed**: our environment is constantly shifting and the athlete, for instance, must shift as well from pre-match talk with the coach to getting on the mat and performing.

Relative to selective attention wrestlers need to focus on the most important aspects of performance at the time. I have consulted with athletes from many different sports and it is amazing where their focus is at times. Athletes have admitted to being focused during the performance on what is for dinner, who they are going out with later, an attractive person in the stands, or what the coach or parents are thinking.

Athletes should breakdown what are the key focal points during their competition. In matches, wrestlers can view stepping on the mat with an opponent as entering a "dome" where nothing outside it matters or exists. The coach may be the only outside focal point that wrestlers attend to when necessary. Otherwise total focus should reside inside the dome.

Maintaining focus over time is also critical. In wrestling the performance is not overly long, but it is intense. Thus, wrestlers must be prepared for short bursts of highly vigorous, battle-like efforts. Focus does not need to be held for a long time, but it must be held intently for the period needed on the mat. Unlike baseball, golf, and many other sports, wrestlers do not have the luxury to relax their focus. Training should mirror the time requirements needed to focus.

While focusing on relevant cues over a period of time is important, so to is the ability to understand the situation. Wrestlers must know time, place, and score so they can appropriately make strategic decisions. There are a number of situations that wrestlers can utilize in Chapter 12.

The fourth way of focusing is to shift focus. Wrestlers have individual ways of preparing for matches. Some are intensely focused while others are loose and joking around five minutes before. The key for all athletes is to recognize when they need to shift their focus from distracting themselves from the situation to keenly focusing on the task at hand. A secondary part of shifting focus is the ability to refocus when distracted. When an athlete is stressing out about how big their opponent is and the fact he is undefeated, he must have the mental capacity to shift focus from his opponent to his own strengths and the game plan.

The ability to concentrate under pressure is certainly a key mental toughness skill that can be trained. In Chapter 3, exercises are presented to train all four ways of focusing as well as methods for refocusing during competitions.

Mental skill wrestling drills for men, women, and children.

Photos by Danielle Hobeika

MENTAL SKILLS TRAINING:
Drills for Wrestling

Larry Lauer, Ph.D. CC-AASP
Director of Coaching Education and Development
The Institute for the Study of Youth Sports
Michigan State University

Chapter Abstract: This chapter contains drills for mental skills that coaches can implement throughout wrestlers' careers. The initial drills are meant to be implemented in the off-season and continued during the pre-season. Later drills are intended to be used throughout the actual season.

Introduction

Up to this point, this book has presented an overview of mental skills, principles regarding their effective use and an emphasis of their importance to learning and performance. If coaches commit to the practical methods for training mental skills as presented here, they will help their wrestlers develop "mental toughness" which is required to execute under pressure, reach their potential and, ultimately, achieve success.

"There are only two options regarding commitment. You're either in or you're out. There's no such thing as life in-between." (Riley, 1993, p. 25).

– Pat Riley, NBA coach

This chapter presents techniques for effectively learning and using all the mental skills previously presented. Mental skills drills are presented as exercises to facilitate this learning and each section concludes with ideas for applying that particular mental skill during competition.

CHAPTER INDEX

Goal-Setting

In the previous chapter, goal-setting was presented as a means to fuel the motivation of wrestlers. Effective goal-setting requires that wrestlers value the goal-setting process and become passionate about achieving their goals. Effective goal-setting also requires introspection on the part of wrestlers in regard to assessing their commitment and an honest self-assessment of their strengths and weaknesses. These assessments form the basis for setting challenging but reachable goals. Achieving these goals, in turn, re-kindles the goal-setting process and increases passion for goal achievement.

Application of Goal-Setting Principles

The goals that wrestlers set through the processes described in this chapter must be based on these principles in order to be effective:

- *Goals* should be written.
- *Both short and long-term* goals should be set and identified as such.
- *Daily goals* should be included as short-term goals.
- *Most goals* should be based on process and performance that lead to the achievement of outcome goals.
- *Wrestlers must realize* that goal-setting is an ongoing process of adjusting and re-setting goals based on progress.
- *Coaches should provide* feedback on progress and wrestlers should seek such feedback.
- *All types of goals* should follow the SMART principles for goal-setting described in the preceding chapter (**S**pecific, **M**easurable, **A**ction-Positive, **R**ealistic, and **T**ime-Frame)

The following drills will help to guide a wrestler to determine his or her wrestling mission. These in turn will serve as a basis for a wrestler to form long-range outcome goals.

3.1 *Banquet Exercise*–Wrestlers Determine What They Value About Wrestling and Themselves

This exercise has wrestlers focus on what is important to them by thinking about what they would like their coach to say about them during the banquet that concludes their senior-year season. In this drill, wrestlers respond to how they would want their coach to present them as an athlete, as a person, and as a teammate.

Wrestlers will read through their answers and highlight the words that reveal the most important things to them. They will identify what stood out, what they discovered about themselves, and what their real aspirations are.

The purpose for this exercise is to have wrestlers recognize their values and goals in regard to themselves as a person and as an athlete.

Example: Colter Johns was one of the most hard working and dedicated wrestlers we ever had here at Scandia High School. He was not the most talented physical wrestler but he put serious time into tactical/technical preparation and excelled in his ability to demonstrate mental toughness. Colter continually worked on setting goals and maintaining focus during practice and competition.

3.2 Wrestlers Interview Five Significant People in Their Life

The purpose of this exercise is to help wrestlers identify their strengths and weaknesses as a person, as an athlete and as a student. In this exercise, wrestlers will interview five people close to them which may include parents, friends, teachers, teammates or coaches.

The five people identified will be asked these questions:
- *What do you see* as my strengths?
- *What areas* do you think I need to improve on as a wrestler?
- *What kind of person* do you think I am?
- *What kind of teammate* do you think I am?
- *What could* I do to improve as a person?
- *What kind of student* do you think I am?
- *How should* I improve as a student?

Wrestlers are to take notes on the answers to these questions and compare responses across those interviewed to identify consistencies. Wrestlers will then compare these responses to their own self-perceptions and use this comparative analysis to determine the self they aspire to become.

3.3 Wrestlers Determine Their Personal Mission

After performing drills #1 and #2, wrestlers have these analyses upon which to base the formation of their personal mission:

1 A list of their values and goals in regard to themselves as a person, as an athlete and as a student.

2 A description of the self they desire to become.

From these analyses, wrestlers will set a mission that could include goals at different time-frames.

For example, their mission might include goals within the following time-frames:

1 Goals they want to achieve **by the end of their wrestling career**.

2 Goals they want to achieve **by the end of graduation**.

3 Goals they want to achieve **the end of the season**.

This mission, and therefore these goals, should address all three categories: academic, personal and wrestling. Wrestlers should again consult significant others while setting their mission.

Wrestlers should also realize that their mission, based on assessments of their progress, must remain dynamic. Sometimes set backs will actually strengthen their mission. Remember, Gable's mission was clear after losing his last NCAA match (e.g. to win the Olympic gold medal).

3.4 Wrestlers Plan to Reach Their Mission

In order to reach their mission, wrestlers, with assistance from their coaches, must create a goal-achievement plan.

This plan should be based on:

- **Thoroughness**
  Includes all three categories of goals: *Outcome, Performance and Process.*

- **Top-Down Planning**
  1st - **Outcome goals**
  2nd - **Performance goals** required to achieving the outcome goals
  3rd - **Process goals** required to achieving the performance goals

In addition, this plan should have:

- **Scope:** realistic limiting of the number of goals
- **Specificity:** clear identification of each goal with the SMART principles applied
- **Sequence:** order in which goals should be achieved–includes short-term goals (daily, weekly) that lead to long-term goals (early-season, mid-season, tournament-time)

Coaches should assist wrestlers in creating their mission achievement plan that follows these principles. In doing so, they should talk to wrestlers about their strengths and weaknesses and have them re-examine their banquet and interview exercises. This will place their focus on the most important things that will help them to achieve their mission. It is better for wrestlers to have five goals that they can put adequate effort into versus 20 goals with insufficient attention to any. Wrestlers should not try to achieve all of their goals at once in order to meet their mission.

Coaches can help wrestlers think of this as climbing a mountain to their mission and identifying the steps they need to take to get there.

Examples of Goals

Outcome Goals:
- *Win* the conference title
- *Win* the district title
- *Place in the regional* meet and thus qualify for the state meet

Performance Goals:
- *Score a takedown* by attacking each side of the opponent with a leg attack in each match
- *Score an escape* using a standup in every match
- *Score a near-fall* with a tilt in each match

Process Goals:
- *Keep head up* on penetration
- *Maintain a strong* base on the bottom to prevent getting broken-down
- *Utilize and perfect* a particular setup (e.g., head tap) to score a leg takedown

Coaches should insist that, each day, wrestlers set two or three performance and/or process goals.

The following are examples of daily practice goals: Wrestlers will

- *Score five single* leg attacks using an arm-drag setup
- *Escape every time* using a standup
- *Work to free* my control arm during my standup attempts at least 70 percent of the time
- *Protect legs* during live wrestling, fending off opponents and resorting to the "funk" no more than three times

The routine of writing down practice goals is time consuming and requires a lot of thought. However, the effort is worthwhile because accomplishing goals enhances the self-confidence of wrestlers. After practice, wrestlers should reflect on that day's performance and set goals for the next day.

Competition Goals

Outcome Goals:
1 Win the match
2 Pin the opponent

Performance Goals:
1 Score at least three takedowns
2 Choose bottom and score a quick escape
3 Score at least one near-fall

Process Goals:
1 Keep head up on penetration
2 Use an arm drag to set up the leg attack
3 Maintain a strong base on the bottom to prevent getting broken down
4 Use a chop-breakdown to capture the opponent's arm in order to score a near fall

Once again, wrestlers should fill out the goal sheet the night before a match (see page 69–at end of the chapter) in order to mentally rehearse the goals by using imagery and positive self-talk before going to sleep at night.

Please read the following example mission and goal strategies.

> **Mission:** I want to be an honor roll student while competing at the 152 pound weight class and qualifying for the state meet
>
> *Example:*
>
> Short term goals to reach mission: Use an arm drag to set up leg attack
>
> Strategy for reaching the goal: Practice arm drag 10 times per practice this week and study at least one hour per night.

Check each goal – is it a SMART goal? Will it fuel the wrestler's motivation?

Now, take each of the goals and list two strategies for achieving it. For example, if your goal is to use an arm drag to set up the leg attack then you could list your strategy as practicing the arm drag at least 10 times per practice.

Taking it to the Mat: Goal Setting

As mentioned previously, application of the SMART principles fuels the wrestler's motivation to achieve goals. In addition, goal-setting must become an intentional daily focus in order to be effective.

In order to help wrestlers get maximum benefit from the goal setting process coaches should:

- *Have wrestlers focus* on two or three goals from their reaching the mission worksheet before practice.
- *Have wrestlers write down* these goals so that they can see them and refer to them during and after practice (maybe using note cards or a goal board in the wrestling room).
- *Have wrestlers make* a concerted effort to achieve their goals in practice and give self-feedback on their progress.
- *After practice,* have wrestlers assess whether or not they achieved each goal, including the identification of reasons why they did or did not achieve them.
- *Have wrestlers identify* and write goals for the next practice or competition. This is when wrestlers adjust their goals based on their current level of success. This may or not require setting new goals. Often, this merely requires a recommitment to the goals that are already established with new strategies for achieving them.

Finally, a great method for recognizing the progress that wrestlers are making is to have wrestlers keep a goal journal. This will help wrestlers track their progress toward their mission.

Journal: Individual Weekly Goals

What am I going to do this week to improve myself as an athlete and as a person and, thereby, help my team be successful?

Weekly Individual Goal Setting		Write yes or no & reason
Date	Goals for the day	Did I meet my goal? Why?

Mentally tough wrestlers exude confidence!

Photo by Al Elrefai

Confidence-Boosting Techniques

"Mentally tough" wrestlers exude confidence and a presence which reflects that they are in control. They believe they will be successful. Opponents and spectators recognize this presence when they step on the mat.

How can wrestlers create this confidence? The first way is to follow the goal-setting process outlined in the previous section.

Once wrestlers have confidence these questions arise:
- *How do they maintain* it under pressure and adversity?
- *When they lose confidence,* how can they regain it?

The answers to these questions require that wrestlers take a "hard look" at themselves. Even the best wrestlers question their confidence at some point which is often the result of some type of harmful thinking.

Wrestler must challenge these patterns of harmful thinking and determine whether they have basis in reality or whether they are unfounded. The following mental skill drill will help wrestlers perform this task.

3.5 Wrestlers Identify and Reframe Their Patterns of Harmful Thinking

It is accepted knowledge that great athletes are confident and that their confidence is linked to the way they perceive themselves and think about themselves. They speak to themselves and to others in confident language that reflects the positive manner in which they think about themselves. When they falter, they reflect on their successful performances, thereby helping them to maintain confidence and overcome temporary failures.

Identifying

> **Directions:** *Complete each statement thinking about the extent to which it describes your thinking.*

Coaches should assure wrestlers that this exercise is simply to help identify any negative thoughts so they can reframe them into positive thoughts.

Pessimism – *The glass is half full. I see the bad side in things, and expect things to not go well*

Not like me	1	2	3	4	5	Like me

Negative Perfectionism – *Things must go perfectly or they are a complete failure*

Not like me	1	2	3	4	5	Like me

Outcome Only – *All that matters is winning, being better than someone else*

Not like me	1	2	3	4	5	Like me

Self-Handicapping – *I predict the outcome before the match, therefore handicapping my chances of success*

Not like me	1	2	3	4	5	Like me

Creating catastrophe – *I blow out of proportion the importance of a situation or losing a match.*

Not like me	1	2	3	4	5	Like me

Poor me – *Things never go right for me, everyone has something against me*

Not like me	1	2	3	4	5	Like me

Entitlement – *I deserve this, it is mine. I should not have to work for what I deserve*

Not like me	1	2	3	4	5	Like me

Unrealistic – *My perception of reality is often "off" and it creates problems for my confidence*

Not like me	1	2	3	4	5	Like me

Past or Future Thinking – *My focus is on past or future events during or before performance, especially when I make a mistake*

Not like me	1	2	3	4	5	Like me

After wrestlers give a score to each type of thinking, coaches should have them list below any of those that were 5's or 4's. Then, coaches should have them identify and list a thought that typifies that kind of thinking and whether it occurs during and/or before competition.

Reframing

Reframing means to adjust a way of thinking to more rational and/or positive thoughts. For example, if a wrestler's thinking does not allow him to accept making mistakes, he will need to challenge that thinking–"Others make mistakes and bounce back, I can too."

Directions: *Make a goal to begin challenging your negative patterns of thinking by reframing them through 2P Thinking; positive and productive.* See the example below.

Reframing Negative Patterns of Thinking into 2P Thinking	
1 Oh boy, I can't win if get taken down first	*Reframe:* One score, big deal. I will escape and score a takedown and go ahead by a point!
2 _____	*Reframe:* _____
3 _____	*Reframe:* _____
4 _____	*Reframe:* _____
5 _____	*Reframe:* _____

Lifestyle: *Positive Affirmations*

After wrestlers identify their patterns of harmful thinking, the next step is to decide what they can do about changing these patterns. Because patterns of harmful thinking are linked to their view of themselves and their world, they become habits that are difficult to change. For example, people who are pessimistic react pessimistically in most aspects of their lives, not just in sport. Pessimism may become a part of their personality making resultant thoughts difficult to overcome.

Athletes do not overcome pessimism just by attempting to think positively during competition. They need to make optimistic thinking a lifestyle change by challenging pessimistic thinking whenever and wherever it occurs–at home, in school, in social settings, at work, and in sport.

One method for wrestlers to overcome their negative patterns of thinking is for them to think about and list their strengths and their positive characteristics. This list might also include their achievements and reasons for their positive relationships with family, friends, and others. Wrestlers can turn these into positive affirmations that serve as reminders that they are well-liked and respected as a person and as an athlete.

Wrestlers can turn these affirmations into a *Positive Thinking for the Day* list which could include five good things about themselves as a person and five good things about themselves as an athlete. Wrestlers should recite their list in the morning and at leisurely intervals during the day. As evidence accrues that these are true characteristics and strengths, a wrestler's self-belief will strengthen.

Another strategy is for wrestlers to list their doubts and then write down how they will overcome each doubt. For example, the doubt could be, "I'm concerned that I will not perform well at states." Then the wrestler draws a line through it and writes beside it, "I will follow this training regimen in order to perform well at states." This is an example of reframing that can become a part of a wrestler's lifestyle.

Saturday Night Live character Stuart Smalley made famous the concept of positive daily affirmations. His tag line of "I'm good enough, I'm smart enough, and doggone it, people like me" is funny but serves to exemplify one point of this section.

Thought-Stopping and Refocusing Routine

For self-limiting beliefs and doubts that may have some basis in reality or doubts that arise during competition, wrestlers may need a more powerful strategy in order to refocus. Developing a thought-stopping routine allows wrestlers to refocus and recreate a positive mindset needed for success.

Coaches can start a thought-stopping process by having wrestlers think about situations that cause them to think negatively and perform poorly. These are *triggers* and wrestlers should identify their negative *triggers* (for example, a slow start, getting taken down and ridden out for the entire first period).

Directions: *List your Triggers*–those situations that cause you to think negatively and cause you to perform poorly.

Trigger *1:* _____

_____

Trigger *2:* _____

_____

Trigger *3:* _____

_____

Coaches should have wrestlers review their *triggers* and describe each of them in as much detail as possible including the situation, individuals involved and their thoughts and feelings. Finally, coaches should have wrestlers clarify how they normally perform in these situations, while attempting to reveal, from start to finish, the what, where, when, how, and why of these performances.

Once the *trigger* situations are described in detail, wrestlers should think about how to stop their harmful thinking that produces these negative reactions. One effective method is to use *Meaningful Cues* in the form of *self-talk* to stop the *trigger*. For example, wrestlers can repeat "stop" when the trigger happens, or "let it go," "move on," "whatever," "ignore it," or "it's no big deal." Another method is to use *visual cues* including seeing a stop sign, a coach holding his hand out as if to say stop, or picturing turning and moving away from the trigger. Some wrestlers may find *physical cues*, such as brushing their leg or wiping their face with a towel as if to wipe it away, to be more effective. Wrestlers can try several methods that they think will work and then choose one that seems to work best and practice it.

Refocusing Cue

Sport psychologists have reported teaching the thought-stopping and refocusing technique to athletes who used the stopping cue but forgot the second step–the refocusing cue. As a result, their negative thinking returned because it was not replaced with a refocusing cue.

For this technique to be effective it must be treated in a two-step fashion: first the stop cue and then the refocusing cue. Refocusing cues are 2P (positive and productive) self-talk used to concentrate on something. For example, if a wrestler becomes highly nervous and doubtful of his chances when he steps on the mat, he will be well advised to "let go" of these thoughts and refocus on "do what you do in practice, you can do this."

Refocusing cues are created by individual wrestlers and need to be different for different trigger situations. The wrestler from the previous example may become angry and filled with thoughts of revenge when he feels an opponent did something illegal (the trigger). He may then begin to take risks and try to go for too much in retaliation. In this trigger situation, the wrestler could still use "let go" as a stopping cue, but then replace it with a 2P (positive & productive) statement of "stay cool, follow the plan."

3.6 Wrestlers Learn to Refocus in "Trigger" Situations

Directions: *At this time list 2P (positive & productive) refocusing statements you think could work that link back to the trigger situations.*

Trigger 1 Refocusing Statement:

    Trigger: Oh darn – I got taken down

    2P Refocus Statement: No biggie-escape and score a takedown myself

Trigger 2 Refocusing Statement:

    Trigger:_____

    2P Refocus Statement:_____

Trigger 3 Refocusing Statement:

    Trigger:_____

    2P Refocus Statement:_____

Excellent, you have given your wrestlers three two-step routines they can use when thinking negatively. They must go out and practice these in training so they become comfortable with using them in competition!

Positive Approach to Mistakes and Losing

Frequently wrestlers struggle after making a mistake or losing a tough match. Their confidence is negatively affected and they may lose trust in their skills. In these tough situations, wrestlers should remember that no one is perfect. Further, the only way they can make their situation better is to learn from the mistake or loss by setting goals to improve and working toward the achievement of these goals. Making mistakes and losing are trigger situations which prompt the use of the thought stopping-refocusing routine presented previously.

If the two-step routine does not work, several other strategies are warranted. Wrestlers can visualize the mistake or loss, erase it from their mind like cleaning off a marker board, and then replace it with positive imagery of successful performances. See the imagery section for more information on how to use imagery.

A second alternate strategy, to be used several hours after the match, is for wrestlers to list the positive and negative aspects of the match. The next morning, wrestlers should review these performance factors and list things they would do differently on the positive list and then discard the negative list. Wrestlers should then review the positive list and incorporate its contents into an imagery session used to set goals for improvement.

Taking it to the Mat: Confidence

In order for wrestlers to be able to apply mental skills in competition, mental skills and routines must be practiced and simulated as realistically as possible in training.

In summary, this includes the following confidence-boosting routines:

- *Identifying* and reframing harmful thinking
- *Positive* affirmation
- *Thought-stopping* and refocusing

Transferring confidence-boosting strategies to the mat requires that wrestlers develop an awareness of triggers and the ability to immediately apply thought-stopping and reframing cues. These abilities must be developed through disciplined practice of these strategies in simulated trigger situations. For example, wrestlers who become negative when they get behind early in matches should practice starting with a deficit and then focus on positive performance cues in order to gain a lead.

Imagery can also be used to enhance confidence. Setting up performance imagery scripts, as well as scripts for responding positively (using the techniques mentioned in this section), can prepare wrestlers to use confidence-boosting techniques and enhance their confidence and readiness to use these techniques.

Arousal And Stress Management

Wrestling is a sport that requires great physical exertion in short bursts, but also the ability to endure very strenuous activity for periods of time. Thus, it is vital that wrestlers manage their arousal and energy levels effectively. If they are unable to do so, they will be inconsistent in their performances. Arousal, in this sense, refers to focus, alertness, and emotional and mental readiness to perform as well as muscle activation.

Energy Thermometer

0° ▬ ▬ ▬ ▬ ▬ ▬ ▬ ▬ ▬ ▬ ▬ ▬ ▬ ▬ ▬ **100°**

10   20   30   40   50   60   70   80   90

Finding an Optimal Level of Arousal: *The Thermometer*

Because energy and arousal are abstract concepts that are hard to calculate, it is not surprising that, when you ask athletes how much energy they need to have to perform, they often cannot give you an answer. Furthermore, athletes often believe that the more arousal the better. Well, this is not the case. Arousal beyond individual optimal levels leads to too much muscular activation and too narrow a focus, both of which interfere with performance.

Photo by Danielle Hobeika

These two wrestlers appear to be optimally aroused and ready for competition.

The simplest way to explain the concept of arousal to athletes is using a thermometer analogy. Remembering from Chapter 2 that arousal activation lies on a continuum from low to high intensity, zero degrees could be considered the energy one has while in a deep sleep. Not much at all. And, the upper end of the thermometer, 100 degrees, could be considered the most energy one has ever experienced. Examples of high activation are when one is startled and adrenaline "kicks in" or when one is experiencing high levels of emotion in emergency situations.

The message here is that, somewhere in between the extremes, there is a temperature range at which athletes perform their best. Athletes should determine the arousal range that leads to their best performances and try to consistently reach that range prior to matches.

3.7 How Hot?

There are two ways to determine optimal level of arousal.

First, have your wrestlers use imagery to recreate their best and worst recent matches. When finished, have them attempt to circle on the thermometer their arousal level in their best match, and place an "X" on their temperature during their worst recent match. This should give them a fairly accurate idea of their optimal level of arousal. Wrestlers are capable of placing a value on their arousal levels if the coach or consultant "walks" them through the process, explains arousal and provides examples of athletes who might fit a certain arousal level. For example, several years ago a mental skills consultant from Penn State University was discussing the arousal levels of some great All-American lightweights at a coaching clinic. He noted that one lightweight had to calm himself to be effective (50-66 degrees on the thermometer) whereas another had to "psych-up" to the point of "bouncing of the wall" (80-90 degrees). This demonstrates that optimal arousal/temperature is an individual phenomenon.

Directions: *If you place your arousal level on a thermometer prior to a match, where would it be?* *What would your temperature be?*

When wrestlers complete this exercise they should have a better idea of the arousal level they need for best performances. However, a more accurate indicator of this optimal range is to take notes on their temperature estimates and corresponding performances. (Along with preparation activities; see the focus/concentration section for more on preparing for matches). These notes will provide wrestlers with data over a number of matches from which they can analyze patterns.

Questions wrestlers should ask themselves are:

- *Is there much fluctuation* in my performance? (A yes answer probably means that their preparation is inconsistent causing inconsistent arousal levels)

- *Comparing their better* and poorer performances, what were the temperatures (i.e., arousal levels)? Is there a consistent temperature range when I am performing well?

- *Again, comparing better* to poorer performances, were there changes in preparation activities? What preparation activities led to my optimal temperature?

Daily Habits Lead to Optimal Arousal for Matches

The arousal level wrestlers bring to the mat is greatly influenced by their off-the-mat lifestyle. Very few wrestlers can live a chaotic, stressful lifestyle and perform with great energy during competition. Wrestlers who are over-aroused often underachieve. Thus, it is important for wrestlers to manage their lifestyle stress levels. Certainly, this will be more difficult for some wrestlers due the nature of their social circumstances.

Minimizing stressful encounters or activities prior to competition is especially important. For example, waiting to study for a big test and then cramming, while in preparation for a meet, is not conducive to controlling one's optimal level of arousal.

Lifestyle Management

A concept that is effective in managing one's daily life is ***TCB:*** *Take Care of Business* to take care of your wrestling. This means that it is important for wrestlers to plan and manage factors and responsibilities in their lives. The factors and responsibilities presented here are *controlling nutrition, managing academics, and planning for recovery.*

Coaches should become educated in regard to nutrition and provide advice to wrestlers in the development of good nutritional habits including planning meals that produce energy from unrefined foods and protein from lean sources. Pre-match meals may require special individual attention.

In regard to managing academics, TCB should take the form of a time-management plan that includes the following:

- *Times and locations* for studying and doing homework
- *Exam dates* with a preparation plan
- *Due dates* for papers and a writing plan
- *Setting personal due dates* and times for the completion of homework, papers and preparation for exams

Following an academic plan can reduce stress, eliminate eligibility worry and lead to higher academic achievement.

While it is important for coaches and wrestlers to apply training, periodization and peaking principles, it is just as important to make sure that rest and recovery are consistently planned and applied. Rest and recovery facilitate the ability of wrestlers to reach their optimal level of arousal prior to matches.

Rest should involve getting ample sleep (at least 7-8 hours) but also consistent sleep (sleep and awake at relatively the same time each day).

Recovery involves much more than rest as recovery activities are aimed at reducing the physical and psychological demands of training and competition. Recovery involves active methods to replenish mental, emotional, and physical resources.

The following recovery methods are suggested here because many athletes have found them to be effective:

- *Getting* a massage
- *Doing progressive* relaxation (see Relaxation section page 48)
- *Doing imagery* (e.g., lying on the beach)
- *Following* a passion outside of wrestling (e.g., playing the guitar)
- *Going* to a nice restaurant with friends
- *Calling* an old friend
- *Doing a light* workout, especially using different activities (e.g., swimming, biking)

Light workouts using different activities create a sense of balance, at least for a short period of time. When wrestlers feel balanced, they feel that they are in control of their lives, thereby enhancing their relaxation and recovery.

3.8 Wrestlers Identify Habits that Raise/ Lower Their Arousal Level

It is important for wrestlers to reflect on their training and competitive de-mands and be aware how these demands are influencing their stress and readiness to compete. Coaches should have wrestlers answer these questions to help gain this awareness.

What habits do I have that lead to a feeling that I am at my optimal level of arousal prior to matches (e.g., consistent sleep, massages)?

What habits do I have that take away from feeling that I am at my optimal level of arousal prior to matches (e.g., cutting weight and unhealthy diet/starving oneself, overtraining the week of a tournament)?

What rest and recovery strategies work for me?

What I will do to have planned recovery?

Minimizing Stress

As discussed earlier, it is important for wrestlers to maintain manageable levels of stress over time in order for them to be consistently energized and ready for competi-tion. Because long-term stress can lead to overtraining, staleness, and even burnout, wrestlers should have plans for rest and recovery and for minimizing potential stress. Wrestlers must be aware of their responses to stress (giving them clues as to when they are experiencing more stress than usual), and be able to apply stress-busting strategies.

Coaches can have wrestlers use the next exercise to identify their signs of stress.

3.9 Wrestlers Identify Their Personal Signs of Stress

Directions: *Check the responses to stress that you typically have.*

- Tension in the muscles increases. _____
- Begin to expect the worst, or "wrestle not to lose." _____
- Focus on things I can't control like the gym temperature or opposing coaches' ranting and raving, instead of thinking about what is happening at the moment! _____
- Narrowing of focus. For instance, focusing on doubts of being successful versus attending to opponent's actions. _____
- Make bad decisions and more likely to lose emotional control and "play dirty." _____

The above list includes some of the most harmful responses to stress. Next is a more comprehensive list of signs and symptoms of stress that coaches and wrestlers should be able to recognize in their self and in others.

Physiological Signs of Stress

- Sweaty palms
- Shallow and rapid breathing
- Frequent trips to the rest room
- Increased heart rate
- Muscle tension
- Butterflies in the stomach

Cognitive Signs of Stress

- Worrying about performance
- Fear of getting injured or re-injured
- Letting the team or coach down
- Inability to focus or concentrate
- Negative self-talk
- Fear of failure
- Worry about meeting other's expectations
- Worry about losing
- Low self-confidence

Behavioral Signs of Stress

- Not sleeping well the night before a contest
- Rushing performance
- Talking when typically quiet
- Pacing
- Drinking more than usual or needed
- Not performing as well in matches as practice

Once wrestlers understand how they typically respond to stress, they can then identify what triggers their stress. Triggers can include the situations, people, feelings, thoughts, and events. The next exercise can help wrestlers to determine what triggers stress in their life and during competition.

3.10 Stress Triggers Reflection

Directions: *Think for a moment about times when you have experienced great amounts of stress.* What happened during that time that overwhelmed you? What was the situation? Who was involved? What thoughts and feelings did you have that might have amplified your stress response? Think of all stresses in your life, including wrestling, and list them.

Stress Source List

_____

_____

_____

_____

_____

Stress-Busting Strategies

While there are many things that wrestlers can do to reduce stress, the most powerful and effective are to ignore stressors or keep them in perspective. While recognizing the necessity of stress to achievement, coaches should help wrestlers learn to respond to stress in positive ways and treat stress (e.g. big matches) as opportunities for success.

While a perspective that minimizes stress is the best preventive strategy, athletes will still experience distress (negative stress). Therefore, it is critical that athletes develop tools or a toolbox of strategies that will help them cope with stress and maintain their optimal level of arousal.

Distinguishing Between Controllable and Uncontrollable Stressors

The first step in developing a "toolbox" of strategies is for wrestlers to distinguish between stressors that they can control and those that they cannot control. For example, because wrestlers cannot control their coach's behavior, they cannot employ a problem-focused coping strategy in response to a stress induced by their coach. In this example, they would need to focus on their response to the stressor or an emotion-focused coping strategy. If, however, the source of stress was feelings of not being fit enough to compete, the problem is under the control of wrestlers who could employ fitness development strategies (problem-focused coping strategies) which, of course, would take time. Therefore, wrestlers would temporarily need to use an immediate "fix" (an emotion-focused coping strategy).

Using Support Sources

Once their stressors have been identified, wrestlers can go to their supporters; those people who will provide encouragement but who will also be willing to provide honest feedback and advice. Thus, it is important for wrestlers to know who they can depend on for support. Knowing that they have supporters gives wrestlers confidence that they will be able to cope with their stress.

3.11 Wrestlers Identify Their Support Sources

Directions: *List the people that you "lean on" (or should "lean on") when you need support*. Then list what kind of support you expect they will provide (encouragement, advice, and challenge).

Supporter and relationship to you	Support that person will provide

"Letting Go" of Stress and Focusing on What is Most Important.

In response to stressful situations, wrestlers often dwell on concerns, doubts, and negative thoughts. Instead, in order to effectively deal with stress, wrestlers need to be able to "let go." While coaches and parents should provide wrestlers with emotional support, they also need to give wrestlers the "personal space" they need to deal with their stressors. After "letting go," wrestlers need to re-focus on immediate stress-reducing solutions.

Taking it to the Mat: Arousal and Stress

The main messages in this section are that wrestlers need to:

1 Learn how to recognize and control their optimal level of arousal.

2 Learn how to recognize stressors and control their stress levels.

An effective method for transferring this knowledge to the mat is for wrestlers to do "check-ins" on their arousal level prior to a match. Wrestlers "check-in" with themselves at predetermined times, such as 45 minutes prior to the match, and ask their self, "What's my temp?" This will create greater awareness of their current arousal level and alert them as to whether they need to relax or energize. This gives wrestlers an opportunity to use their "mental toughness" skills to control their optimal level of arousal by match-time.

Relaxation

Relaxation: *Preparation, and Routines*

There are many ways to relax and reduce stress including yoga, meditation, tai chi, deep breathing, and muscular relaxation. Relaxation routines can be used to reduce stress in preparation for a match, during a match and after a match.

In Chapter 2, the importance of relaxation was emphasized. Relaxation was defined as a physical and mental response of peacefulness and calmness. This includes reducing tension level, "clearing one's head," lowering the heart rate, decreasing the rate of breathing, and creating a feeling of calmness.

The understanding that optimal levels of arousal are individually different has also been discussed. Regardless of whether wrestlers' optimal arousal levels are high or low, they still need to learn to guard against over-arousal through relaxation techniques.

"Quality" Relaxation starts with the Right Environment and Deep Breathing

It is critical that wrestlers seriously practice the correct techniques of relaxation exercises in order for these techniques to transfer to competitive situations.

In order for wrestlers to "buy into" using relaxation techniques for competition, it is important that they experience success during relaxation practice in terms of feeling comfortable, calm, quiet and focused. Therefore, the environment for relaxation practice should be low stress with minimal distractions in order for wrestlers to be able to focus on technique.

When relaxation is practiced as a team, coaches need to request seriousness and explain its benefits for competition. Coaches should ask wrestlers to focus as they would on the mat and provide clear directions for the exercise. This should include having them get into a comfortable position by removing tension–arms at the side, legs not crossed, shoulders relaxed, etc. Wrestlers should be reminded that the goal is to experience a calm, quiet, relaxed state which will benefit them if duplicated in competition.

Most relaxation techniques are effective when wrestlers are able to slow down and be quiet. This is why it is beneficial to teach deep breathing first, and then the other more advanced techniques that require calmness-imagery, centering, and progressive relaxation.

Deep breathing involves slow, rhythmic breathing by expanding the abdomen instead of the chest during inhalation (often called "belly breathing"). The easy way to explain it is for coaches to have their wrestlers put their hands on their navel and then inhale attempting to comfortably (not forcefully) push out their navel and their hand. Coaches should explain to wrestlers that breathing from the abdomen brings more oxygen into the body and slows their breathing which, in turn, reduces feelings of anxiety and stress and allows them to recover faster.

3.12 Wrestlers Learn How to Use Deep Breathing Tools

When learning deep breathing, it is important for wrestlers to breathe in through the nose to a count of three, and out through the mouth to a count of five. In this manner, wrestlers will extend, but not force, the exhalation phase. In order to control the timing during the teaching of deep breathing, coaches may want to count for them in a very slow, quiet, and calm manner so that wrestlers learn the appropriate rhythm. Coaches could also use a metronome to assist in controlling wrestlers' breathing rhythm.

- Get into a comfortable position.
- Inhale deeply and slowly through the nose for 3 seconds.
- Fill the stomach (abdomen) with air instead of the chest.
- Exhale slowly from the mouth for 5 seconds.
- Count 1, 2, 3 (inhale); 1, 2, 3, 4, 5 (exhale) to develop a rhythm.
- As you exhale, say a word that will help you relax like "cool," "chill," or "calm."
- Continue deep breathing 5-10 minutes.

When this exercise is finished, coaches should ask their athletes about what they experienced by asking these questions: Was it a calming sensation? Were they able to clear out distractions and focus only on counting and the feel of breathing—the rising and falling of the abdomen? Eventually, the goal will be for wrestlers to obtain a relaxed feeling prior to competition and, possibly, during competition.

Progressive Relaxation Cycles and Muscle Groups

An excellent method for reducing tension, calming nerves, and reducing pressure is muscular relaxation. Athletes often appreciate this more physical form of relaxation because they can feel a difference between the tense and relaxed states. A popular method of muscular relaxation is using controlled, deep breathing with Jacobsen's Progressive Muscular Tense-Relaxation. In this method, wrestlers do deep breathing to get into a relaxed state. Then, wrestlers first tense a muscle or muscle group during inhalation to a count of three, and then they release that tension as they exhale to a count of five while noticing the changes from tension to relaxation.

Wrestlers should not expect immediate performance results from incorporating progressive relaxation because it is a skill mastered only through repetitive and systematic practice over time.

In order to learn how to do progressive relaxation, athletes should go through these four phases of training:

Phase 1: Tense-Relax Cycle – tense and relax various muscle groups throughout the body focusing on the feelings associated with tensed and relaxed states. Time: 3-4 days; 10-20 minutes a day.

Phase 2: Relaxation Only Cycle – relax muscle groups individually without tensing.

Begin to use a cue word such as "relax" or "let go" or image (e.g., water flowing slowly down a river) to signal relaxation. Time 7 days; 5-10 minutes a day.

Phase 3: Full-Speed Relaxation Cycle – learn to relax individual muscle groups more quickly. The ultimate goal is to learn to relax deeply in the time it requires to take a deep breath, inhale and exhale slowly. Time: 7 days; 20 times per day.

Phase 4: Utilization Cycle – begin to use relaxation in stressful situations. Practice relaxation first under low stress conditions (e.g., in practice during drills), then under moderately stressful conditions (e.g., scrimmages), and finally employ relaxation under highly stressful conditions (e.g., just before stepping on the mat).

After learning to relax each muscle individually, wrestlers should group muscles together for the purpose of relaxing larger portions of the body.

Directions: *Use the following table to speed up the relaxation process in the final days of Phase 1.*

7 Muscle Groups	4 Muscle Groups	2 Muscle Groups
Hands	Arms and hands	
Arms		
Face	Face and neck	Upper body (abdomen and up)
Neck		
Chest/shoulders/upper back	Chest/shoulders/back and abdomen	Lower body (hips and down)
Lower back/abdomen		
Legs and feet	Legs and feet	

It may be possible for wrestlers who have a good feel for relaxation, to start with the seven-muscle group program. Wrestlers should use the program that is most effective for them in obtaining a relaxation response. Then they can progressively move to two-and four-muscle groups until they are able to relax the whole body with one or just a few breaths. At first, a relaxation session may require 20 minutes. But later, when wrestlers have achieved one breath relaxation, the session is only seconds long.

Progressive muscular relaxation should be practiced in a quiet and dark environment without potential for distractions.

Such an environment facilitates wrestlers' ability to comply with the following directions:
- *Get into a comfortable position* by lying down without a pillow, arms to your sides and your legs straight.
- *Begin deep breathing* to develop a single mental focus.
- *Develop a passive attitude* as you breathe deeply allowing "noise" to come into your thoughts and then float away.
- *Tense and relax each muscle* in the body starting with the toes and ending at the scalp.
- *Tense each muscle* for three seconds as you inhale, and then relax it for five seconds as you exhale.
- *Do each muscle* three times or until fully relaxed.
- *During the relaxation* cycle focus on the tension leaving the muscle.
- *Notice the difference* between the tense and the relaxed state.
- *Use a cue word* that will help you to the relax (e.g., calm, relax, flow, loose, etc.)
- *Your cue word* will act as a trigger for later relaxation in a stressful environment.

Relaxation Script for Novice Wrestlers

The following script is an effective exercise to use with younger wrestlers. It will give them an early introduction to ways to relax for competition. It is reprinted by permission from Terry Orlick.

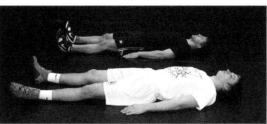

Photo by Haley Conn

Spaghetti Toes

There are lots of games you can play with your body. We'll start with one called Spaghetti Toes. I wonder how good you are at talking to your toes. I'll bet you are pretty good. Let's find out.

Tell the toes on one of your feet to wiggle. Are they wiggling? On just one foot? Good! Now tell those toes to stop wiggling. Tell the toes on your other foot to wiggle. Tell them to wiggle real slow…and faster….and real slow again…slower…stop! Did your toes listen to your instructions? Good. If you talk to different parts of your body, as you just did with your toes, your body will listen to you especially if you talk to them a lot. I'm going to show you how you can be the boss of your body by talking to it.

First, I want to tell you something about spaghetti, I like spaghetti. I bet you do, too. But did your ever see spaghetti before it's cooked? It's kind of cold and hard and stiff, and it's easy to break. When it's cooked, it's warm and soft and kind of lies down and curls up on your plate.

I want to see if you can talk to your toes to get them to go soft and warm and sleepy like cooked spaghetti lying on your plate. You might have to talk to them quite a bit to make them know what you want them to do, but I know they can do it.

Wiggle your toes on one foot. Now tell these toes to stop wiggling. Tell them to go soft and sleepy like warm spaghetti lying on your plate. Now wiggle the toes on your other foot. Stop wiggling. Turn those toes into soft spaghetti. Good.

Now wiggle one leg. Stop wiggling. Tell the leg to go soft and sleepy like warm spaghetti. Now wiggle the other leg. Stop. Tell it to go soft and sleepy. Wiggle your behind. Let it go soft and sleepy.

Wiggle your fingers on one hand. Tell your fingers to stop wiggling. See if you can make those fingers feel warm and sleepy like spaghetti lying on your plate. Now wiggle your fingers on your other hand. Slowly. Stop. Make those fingers feel warm. Tell them to go soft and sleepy. Now wiggle one arm. Stop. Tell your arm to go soft and sleepy. Now wiggle the other arm and tell it to go soft and sleepy. Good.

Try to let your whole body go soft and warm and sleepy, like soft spaghetti lying on your plate. [Pause] That's really good. Your body is listening well. Let your body stay like spaghetti and just listen to me. I want to tell you about when spaghetti toes can help you.

When you are worried or scared of something, or when something hurts, your toes and your hands and muscles get kinda hard and stiff—like hard spaghetti before it's cooked. If you are worried, scared, or something hurts you, you feel a lot better and it doesn't hurt so much if your hands and toes and muscles are warm, soft spaghetti lying on a plate. If you practice doing spaghetti toes, you'll get really good at it. Then you can tell your hands and toes and muscles to help you by going warm and soft and sleepy, even if you are scared or something hurts.

Before you go, let's try talking to your mouth. Wiggle your mouth. Let it go soft and sleepy. Wiggle your tongue. Let it go soft and sleepy. Wiggle your eyebrows. Let them go soft and sleepy. Let your whole go warm and soft and sleepy. Let your whole feel good. (Orlick, 1992, p. 325).

– Terry Orlick, Positive Living Skills: Joy and Focus for Everyone *(2011)*
General Store Publishing House (pgs 173- 176) www.gsph.com

Spaghetti toes can be used to help youth wrestlers relax and control their nerves.

Photo by Danielle Hobeika

Centering

Eventually, wrestlers should strive to be able to relax in a short amount of time–30 seconds or less. Because the competitive environment presents wrestlers with a burst of anxiety as their name is being called or the national anthem is being played, they need to be able to breathe and gain the relaxation response quickly. Also, wrestlers will not be lying on the floor and relaxing for 10 minutes right before they step on the mat. Therefore, wrestlers should be taught how to center. Centering brings the exercise of deep breathing into a more active state. It is equatable to the one-breath relaxation goal of muscular relaxation as previously presented.

After they have learned and mastered deep breathing and/or progressive relaxation, wrestlers should practice deep breathing in their athletic stance and in different competitive situations.

The keys to centering for wrestlers are:

1 Focus on their core, their center of balance, their self.

2 Bring their attention inward and focus on feeling calm, strong, balanced, and ready.

Wrestlers usually feel ready to compete when this process is completed. This centering tools provides the instructions for this mental skill.

3.13 Wrestlers Learn How to Use Centering Tools

- Get into an athletic ready stance.
- Inhale deeply and slowly through the nose for 3 seconds.
- Take a deep belly breath instead of a shallow chest breath.
- Focus on your strength—your center of gravity.
- Exhale slowly from the mouth for 3 seconds.
- As you exhale say a word that will help you relax like "cool," "chill," or "calm."

Centering, like other mental skills in this chapter, should be trained over time. Athletes should not expect to effectively use centering without practicing for some time.

Taking it to the Mat: Relaxation

It is important that relaxation transfer to competitive situations. Wrestlers should practice centering and deep breathing in different training situations. For example, wrestlers can prepare to wrestle an opponent in practice by using centering just before stepping on the mat. Simulation could also occur against less skilled, equally skilled and superior opponents. The objective is for centering to become a habit that will transfer to competition.

However, this transfer occurs only if wrestlers intentionally practice centering and make it a part of their pre-match routine. Wrestlers should use centering right before the start of a match and/or before each period. Also, after an out-of-bounds situation, wrestlers should to take a deep breath and one total body contraction while centering on the job at hand (scoring a takedown, escape, reversal, or near fall—whatever the situation dictates) as they return to center mat. Most importantly, wrestlers should be taught to use centering for self-control after adversity in a match (e.g. after a perceived bad call, losing a late lead). Coaches can purposely make bad calls in practice matches to simulate a situation that requires centering.

When it's match-time, wrestlers need to feel prepared, relaxed, and confident. Centering is a great method for achieving these feelings.

Imagery

Imagery is a powerful tool that, if used correctly, can provide an important mental edge for wrestlers. However, as described in Chapter 2, many athletes often have negative experiences with imagery. Often, these negative imaging experiences occur automatically, usually as a result of feelings of anxiety and doubt. Certainly, positive imaging experiences may also occur automatically.

Because imaging experiences will occur automatically whether they are controlled or not, the key is for wrestlers to learn to control their imaging so that they receive only positive "movies in their mind"–those that will enhance their confidence, their focus and, consequently, their performance. Wrestlers can gain control of their imagery by practicing it and having a plan for using it at opportune times.

Imagery practice must be performed in the right environment with correct methods. The practice of watching "movies in their mind" can be accomplished either by wrestlers imagining the actual experience through their own eyes or by imagining themselves in a movie. Wrestlers should use imagery during practice after seeing a particular move demonstrated and just prior to rehearsing particular moves. There are several ways to take advantage of this powerful tool.

How to practice imagery: *Creating a Conducive Environment*

Controllability and vividness are the two important aspects of imagery. It is important that the imaging environment be conducive for wrestlers to successfully control vivid images and, as a result, enhance their confidence in the technique.

The characteristics of the imaging training environment should be the same as those for relaxation training. For beginners, a quiet, dark environment with no distractions works best. Coaches should require silence in group settings. As wrestlers' imaging improves, they can progressively learn to ignore distractions. This gives wrestlers the opportunity to totally engage in the imagery experience.

The imagery process should include the following procedures:
Wrestlers will -
- *Plan the content* of the imagery beforehand.
- *Get into a comfortable* position in order to relax.
- *Do deep breathing* for 3-5 minutes or until their mind is focused.
- *Imagine their* planned images.
- *Focus on their feelings* created by the images–confidence, focus, control, composure, readiness.
- *Use the imagery tools* and remember to try to involve all their senses to create images that feel real.

3.14 Wrestlers Learn How to Use Imagery Tools

Goal: *See what you want to prepare for matches and boost your confidence*

Steps:

- Think first before starting about what you want to visualize.

- Then, start with deep breathing to clear your head (usually 3-5 minutes).

- Once your head is clear, picture the images you want.

- Focus on the feelings of confidence, calmness, composure and readiness you gain from the visualization.

- If you see negative or irrelevant images, try the following:

  - Go to a black screen and then refocus on your image.

  - Take the remote and change the channel in your head to the positive image.

  - Erase it on the marker board, and then replace it.

What Should Wrestlers Image?

What should wrestlers focus on during imagery? This is a common question, the answer to which is determined by the goal or purpose of the imagery.

For learning and practicing, wrestlers should select simple images such as an inanimate object (e.g., the mat, the gym), and memorable images (e.g., a favorite vacation or favorite locale). In the beginning stages, wrestlers should avoid visualizing very much movement or a changing environment. Limiting the images at first will enhance their ability to learn image control. Wrestlers new to imagery, should focus on previous experiences as opposed to trying to create a future event (such as competing at nationals). As wrestlers improve, they can create more complex images that move (e.g., competing, practicing a move, the rival's gym prior to the match).

It is important for wrestlers to imagine the feelings that correspond with their mental pictures of successful techniques. Combining emotions with visuals make the imagery experience real. Examples of feelings that wrestlers may want to create include self-assurance, pride, domination and relaxed control. Wrestlers should identify and use "power" cues with images that help them to establish the feelings they want to create such as "confidence," "control," "aggressive," "fast," "explode," etc.

3.15 Wrestlers Identify Their Purposes for Using Imagery

Directions: *List below the purposes for using imagery.* Then, list the "power" cues and images that can be recreated to achieve these purposes.

Example:

Purpose: To practice control of images

> *Power Cues/Images:* The mat

Purpose: To relax

> *Power Cues/Images:* A vacation at the beach

Purpose: To feel prepared for competition

> *Power Cues/Images:* "Confident," "Ready," image preparation routine going well

Purpose: _____

> *Power Cues/Images:* _____

Purpose: _____

> *Power Cues/Images:* _____

Purpose: _____

> *Power Cues/Images:* _____

Purpose: _____

> *Power Cues/Images:* _____

Specific Uses of Imagery

Imaging for technique: the when

The best times to practice imagery for learning technique are:

- *Before practice* to imagine techniques that wrestlers know they will be practicing
- *During practice* right before actually executing the technique
- *At the end of practice* coaches can plan a team-reflection period as the last part of practice
- *Just before* going to sleep at night

Imaging for technique: the how

Wrestlers can watch themselves going through moves from the day's practice. For instance, if wrestlers were introduced to a circle arm-drag setup into a single leg takedown on someone who reaches to block them, they would see and feel this move in slow motion. They would see the opponent reach to block their arm and see themselves complete a circular motion with their hand and reach for the opponent's armpit to complete the drag.

Mentally tough wrestlers are able to eliminate distractions such as injury or fatigue.

Photo by Danielle Hobeika

Dealing with adversity

A powerful use of imagery is to see one's self dealing with adversity and then bouncing back successfully. For example, a slightly injured wrestler could imagine being in pain and his opponent attacking his injured knee. Then, he could imagine thinking "Doesn't hurt. I can do this stay focused" and follow his game plan with power and control.

Wrestlers should have a well-developed routine for dealing with adversity so that they can imagine it and feel like they have control of adverse situations (e.g., thought stopping and refocusing routine).

Troubleshooting: *What to do When Imagery is Not Working*

When imagery is not going well for wrestlers, their flow of positive images and feelings will be intermittently interfered with by negative pictures and feelings. Wrestlers will not see what they want to see nor will they feel what they want to feel. Wrestlers then need to analyze their interferences and regain control.

The following procedures will help them to accomplish this:

1 *Clear your head* by using deep, controlled breathing until you are focused on counting your breaths, then focus on one word or one image, and then, begin imagery.

2 *Try not to force* your imagery. When distractions enter, let them float away to avoid getting frustrated. It is natural for thoughts to "jump around," so do your best to stay focused but know that you will get distracted at times.

3 *When your imagery* is not going well and you are seeing negative things, stop and restart. Do this by visualizing a "black screen," erasing the negative image from a marker board, or symbolically taking the remote control and changing the channel to a positive image.

4 Make sure you have eliminated daily distractions from your imagery environment. Play calming music in the background if you need some consistent noise to focus on.

5 Try something easier to visualize like your home, the mat, a memorable vacation spot, etc.

Imagery Plan

Because imagery will not improve without continued practice, wrestlers need to train imagery in a progressive fashion. The recommendation here is to practice three to four times per week, especially at the beginning stage. Beginners should start with simple control and use the vividness scripts provided below. As wrestlers improve, they can change scripts, create different scripts or add more difficult images. Regardless of what scripts are used wrestlers should monitor their success.

Scripts for Practicing Control and Vividness:

Listed next are two imagery scripts to practice as a way to improve your imagery control and vividness. After mastering these, change them and add content from your own experience (such as the environment at the conference tournament).

Clarity Script

Imagine walking out of the locker room and opening the door to the wrestling room. Notice the change in temperature. Take a deep breath and smell the mat, the sweat, and other surroundings. As you walk around the outside of the big circle on the mat notice how you feel; excited, energized, confident, ready, in control, skilled. Feel how light your shoes feel as you skip on the mat to warm. Is the mat rock hard or is it spongy. Is it wet or slippery from just being mopped? Now look around the room. Look at circles on the mat for practice scrimmages, the lines on the mat for up-down starts, the quotes on the walls, and the lights on the ceiling. In your mind's eye, create an image of the wrestling room.

With Success, Progress to…

Become aware of other wrestlers on the mat warming up. See some of them jogging/skipping in a circle to warm-up as others are beginning to shadow drill. Begin to drill with a partner to warm up–duck-under, single leg, double leg. Feel your muscles work and your body begin to warm-up. Hear the thump of the mat as you bring your partner to the mat. Feel the partners' kneepad as you shoot a single leg. Hear your teammates and the coaches talking. Finally, focus on the feelings you have as you warm-up.

3.16 Control Script

Imagine yourself standing center mat. Examine it very closely: the color of the mat, the color of the lines and the texture of the mat and any other parts you can imagine. Were you able to conjure a detailed image of the mat from your mind? Now see an opponent standing across from you. What is the color of his singlet? What about the referee, is he short or tall? Imagine that you are waiting for the whistle to start the match. Imagine yourself waiting to shake hands with your opponent. What did the grip feel like? See and hear the whistle blow to start the match. Feel the mat as you lower your level and attack a single leg. You feel your opponent's leg as you capture it with a good angle. Feel your self quickly and powerfully scoring on your opponent as the referee signals for a two-point takedown.

Once wrestlers have experience with imagery and can control it, they can begin to develop individual plans that target specific purposes for doing the imagery (e.g. imagining execution of a match-plan or a move, etc.). This is a sample pre-meet script that could be adapted to specific situations and preferences.

Pre meet scripts *(example)*

First period: I will attack using an inside bicep tie to force the action and set up my double-leg attack. I will push pull and fake shots until I see the opening to lower my level and penetrate. Once I capture the legs I will immediately change direction and drive across his body with my head up. I will keep driving until I get him to the mat and will look for a pinning-combination as we hit the mat.

Second period: I will defer or take the down position. At the whistle, I will explode up clearing my arm and getting hand control. If needed, I will hip-in and out to score my escape. Then it is back to takedowns.

Third period: I should be ahead by at least three points and will work a high half nelson to work for a fall.

Taking it to the Mat: **Imagery**

After wrestlers are comfortable and confident with using imagery, they will want to advance to using imagery in competition. Competition plans should include purposes (see previous exercise on the Purposes of Imagery on page 56) and content. For instance, a wrestler could use imagery as a part of a routine to use after making a mistake ("let it go," deep breath, imagine making a successful execution). Next is a planning worksheet for training and using imagery successfully.

3.17 Wrestlers Create Their Plan for Training and Using Imagery

In order for imagery to be useful, it must be practiced regularly and implemented in preparation and performance. List below how you will train imagery and use it to wrestle with more confidence, readiness, and focus.

I will train my imagery by (how many days per week/how long; when, where, what?):

I will use imagery to prepare by (during your preparation for a match, when will you use it, where, and what will you imagine?):

In competition I will use imagery when (in what situations could imagery help you stay committed, focused, or bounce back from adversity?):

Focus And Concentration

Concentration is paying total attention by focusing mental effort on external and internal events.

This involves four distinct kinds of focusing:
- **Selective attention:** focusing on the most relevant cues
- **Maintaining focus:** over the time needed to perform
  (i.e. the duration of a match, during a tournament, etc.)
- **Situational awareness:** understanding time, place, score, etc.
- **Making decisions accurately:** based on current information
- **Shifting focus as needed:** our environment is constantly shifting and the athlete, for instance, must shift as well from pre-match talk with his coach to getting on the mat and performing.

Factors that facilitate the ability to focus, have been presented in previous sections of this chapter. Confident wrestlers are better able to quiet their mind and focus which, in turn, increases the effectiveness of other mental drills wrestlers may wish to use. These mental drills should be a part of a preparation plan for competition.

Identifying Focal Points and Distractions

It is crucial that coaches understand all their wrestlers' focal points and distractions in order to help them develop individualized plans for focusing and refocusing.

3.18 Wrestlers Identify Their Focal Points

What should wrestlers focus on leading up to competition? What activities, tasks, and events will help them get ready for competition? While there are certainly many possibilities, coaches can have their wrestlers think about their best recent match and review the details of how they prepared.

Focal Points in Preparation for Matches		
	Best Match	**Worst Match**
The day before competition	Saw myself executing perfect technique	Had bad practices and carried over to my images
The morning of competition	Had a great breakfast—felt energized-great thoughts	Sucked too much weight, too fast
During the ride to the site	High energy snack–ready to perform	Felt sick and out of shape
At the site	Made weight easy–ready to execute perfect technique	I felt weak
The last hour prior to the match	My mind is right! Ready to go—body feels great	I am so tired
Final preparation (last few moments prior to match)	I am sweating–great warm up—ready to go!	Warm up sucked—feel so tired from cutting weight

Coaches can then have their wrestlers reflect on their distractions. Obviously, in the sample above, "making weight" is the big distraction for that wrestler. However, there are so many other distracting possibilities including school work, family relationships, girlfriends, financial problems, etc. The identification of their distraction will help wrestlers learn about themselves and enable them to create methods of effective preparation for competition.

3.19 Wrestlers Identify Their Distractions

What things take me off of my preparation focus?

What would I prefer to not do in the last 24 hours prior to competing?

Establishing a Preparation Plan for Optimal Focus

Once wrestlers have identified their focal points and distractions, they are ready to create their preparation plan for matches. Their first step in doing so should be to review their responses to the Focal Points and Distractions exercises. Then they should respond to the following readiness questions.

Exercise: **Are you ready?**

Now think about how your preparation is helping/hurting your performance.

Are you ready at the start of the match on a consistent basis (90% of matches)?

- Physically (energized, but not stressed out and tight)?

- Mentally (focused on the match; positive and productive in your thinking)?

- Do you start quickly?

- Do you have the right amount of energy?

- Are you focused?

- Are you confident?

- Are you in control of your emotions?

If wrestlers answer "no" to any of these questions, they should analyze their preparation and find ways to enhance it. For instance, if they have trouble starting quickly, they may need to reflect on their readiness and incorporate an energizing activity, a relaxation technique or an imagery experience in order to better prepare. Knowing what distracts them helps wrestlers to identify and incorporate effective mental skills into their preparation routines.

Wrestlers should list the activities, tasks, and events that should occur in their preparation during the 24 hours leading up to competition. Wrestlers should be very specific about these events. For example, instead of writing "I will focus" write "I will focus by doing 15 minutes imagery consisting of making my moves with ease, confidence, and power."

3.20 Wrestlers Create a Pre-Match Preparation Plan

	Physical Activities	Mental Activities
Day Before		
Ride to Match		
At the Site		
Last Hour Before Match		
Final Moments Before Match		

Once wrestlers create a preparation plan, they should follow it consistently and chart how it is working (see Post Match Analysis on page 69-70). Wrestlers should be advised not to discard their plan when they experience a bad match. Instead, they should give their plan ample testing time until it becomes obvious that changes should be made.

Pre-Match Refocusing Routines

While wrestlers should always have a match-preparation plan, unexpected factors often interfere. Common factors are those that interfere with the event time schedule such as transportation problems for teams or for officials. Timing during tournaments is especially uncontrollable (often due to matches that end in early falls or overtime matches). Wrestlers should attempt to anticipate these issues and develop refocusing routines to adjust and compensate. For example, if the bus arrives late and the team now has only 35 minutes to prepare each wrestler should know what parts of warm-up will be eliminated and focus on the most vital aspects of preparation. They may also shorten some activities such as doing five minutes of imagery instead of 15. Unexpected events can be simulated in practices or scrimmages in preparation for real occurrences.

Refocusing routines should have three-steps:
- *Respond* in a positive way (e.g., "oh, the bus is late. Ok I have a plan for that, let me review it.")
- *Relax* (e.g., do some imagery and deep breathing while on the bus and running behind versus getting uptight)
- *Refocus* (e.g., review the short warm-up and know what you will do on site, remind yourself to prepare for this to happen).

Distracting Events Refocusing Routine

Directions: ***Wrestlers should plan ahead to deal with such issues using the 3R refocusing routine.*** There are several situations which may cause distractions for a wrestler. Distracting scenarios might include getting to the gym late, not making weight until the last minute, having an equipment issue, or lineup changes.

Example: Suddenly start getting tight and worried about the result.

> **Respond:** "Let it go"

> **Relax:** Imagery of successful past performance

> **Refocus:** Cues as warming up, "You can do this, you are ready."

3.21 Wrestlers Develop Focal Points

In-Match Focus and Refocusing Routines

While much effort has been spent on preparing for matches, it is important that coaches look at what wrestlers should do during the match itself.

A match can be segmented into two parts:

1 When there is action.

2 When there is a break.

During the breaks, wrestlers should plan a focus so that will help them to be ready for immediate further action. There are also particular focal points that wrestlers should focus on during action. These focal points need to be individually determined and planned by wrestlers. Wrestlers can use the next exercise to identify focal points they experienced during their best and worst matches.

Photo by Danielle Hobeika

Deep breath, no distraction...
Focusing on the next score!

Focal Points During a Match		
	Best Match	**Worst Match**
During breaks:	What my next move would be	Thinking about how strong the opponent was
During the actual wrestling:	Checking for openings to score and doing it	I am getting embarrassed...
During the ride to the site:	Watched movies—relaxed	Thinking about how tough the guy was supposed to be

Once the Focal Points During a Match exercise are identified, Distraction During a Match should also be identified..

Directions: *Identify your distractions during a match.*
What things take you off of your in-match focus?

Distractions During a Match	
During breaks:	Checking out the cheerleaders
During the actual wrestling:	Thinking about being out of shape and how tired I am
During the injury time out:	Thinking about the test I failed

Knowing these focal points and distractions allows wrestlers to:
1 *Plan to set focal point* reminders that trigger a strong focus.
2 *Recognize how they* become distracted.

An example of using a trigger could be tapping the floor right before action as a reminder to give 100 percent effort. An example of overcoming being distracted by the crowd could be to keep looking at the mat only while using a refocusing routine ("eyes on mat," centered breathing, "let's go!").

After reflecting on the disruptions to match focus, wrestlers will find it helpful to use a 3Rs routine - respond positively, relax and refocus. Coaches should have wrestlers develop routines that will help them regain their focus because it is impossible to sustain focus for the course of a whole match.

3.22 Wrestlers Create In-Match 3R Routine Response, Relax, Refocus

Photo by Danielle Hobeika

Wrestlers refocus after going out of bounds.

Distraction: Taken down

Response: "Let it go" with brushing off motion

Relax: Centered breathing

Refocus: "Follow the plan, you will do this."

Distraction 3 Rs Routine

_____

_____

_____

Wrestlers do not need more than two or three refocusing routines. Having only a few routines will allow wrestlers to master them. Many of these routines are similar with just small differences. For example, wrestlers can learn to remind themselves to "focus" regardless of the nature of the distraction.

Taking it to the Mat: The Plan and a Practice Log

Becoming "mentally tough" on the mat does not happen accidentally. Wrestlers must have a monitoring plan for developing and adapting mental skills through training.

Directions: *Coaches should have wrestlers select 2-3 mental skills goals* areas of their mental game they want to improve. Next, coaches should work with each wrestler individually to come up with ways to practice these mental skills (many ideas have been provided in this chapter).

Three Mental Skills Goals

1. _____

   _____

2. _____

   _____

3. _____

   _____

How I will Practice these Mental Skills?

1. _____

_____

2. _____

_____

3. _____

_____

The next step for coaches would be to monitor each wrestler's "mental toughness" training through a weekly log. In today's tech-savvy world they could be completed on-line with only the coach and athlete having access.

Mental Toughness Skills Practice Log			
Date	Mental Toughness Skill	How I Practiced It	Success(1–bad, 2–ok, 3–good)
Example:			
6/1/2010 Monday	Relaxation	Muscle relaxation 15 minutes at home before bed	Became relaxed and less tense was able to clear head of distractions, was a 3

3.23 Wrestling Match Goal Form

Photo by Danielle Hobeika

Wrestlers should evaluate the good, the bad, and the ugly after every match using this wrestling match goal form.

It's Time To Wrestle

Once wrestlers have engaged in mental skills training and have completed their pre-season tactical/technical preparation the time for competition has arrived. Coaches should use the Wrestling Match Goal Form to set match goals, and evaluating the goals after the match. Remember to have the wrestlers focus on process and performance goals versus strictly outcome goals. Remind wrestlers to focus on the SMART goal setting process.

The competitive reflection section of the Wrestling Match Goal Form will allow coaches to work with wrestlers on their individual strengths and weaknesses. Coaches and parents should be reminded that this form is never to be used to compare wrestler A with wrestler B or to decide who should make the lineup for a particular match. It is only to be used to compare a particular wrestler with themselves and to improve aspects of mental skill such as arousal, focus, determination, and/or mental game-planning.

This form can be used for pre-match goals and post-match evaluation. See Appendix on page 276 for form to copy and use.

Pre-Match
- *What are your two performance* or process goals for this match?
- *What are your strategies* for achieving those goals?
- *How will you know* if you have achieved your goals?

Post-Match

To what degree did you meet goal #1?

Didn't meet my goal   Completely met my goal

1	2	3	4	5	6	7	8	9	10

To what degree did you meet goal #2?

Didn't meet my goal   Completely met my goal

1	2	3	4	5	6	7	8	9	10

Competition Reflections

Circle your feelings going into and during the match:

No confidence in my physical preparation	1	2	3	4	5	Completely confident in my physical preparation
Did not execute strategy or plan at all	1	2	3	4	5	Completely executed strategy or plan
Very distracted, not able to block out distractions	1	2	3	4	5	Completely focused, blocked out distractions
Did not cope well with pain, factors outside of my control	1	2	3	4	5	Coped well with pain, factors outside of my control
Did not have a clear sense of purpose for match	1	2	3	4	5	Had a strong sense of purpose for match
No determination	1	2	3	4	5	Completely determined
Very worried	1	2	3	4	5	No worries at all
No physical activation (flat)	1	2	3	4	5	Highly physically activated (positive)
No commitment to push myself	1	2	3	4	5	Completely committed to push myself

**What were at least two things that went well?
**What were two things that did not go as well as you would have liked?

Taking It To The Mat: Match Goal-Setting And Competitive Reflections

Coaches must make the use of the Wrestling Match Goal Form a regular part of the pre and post-match process or it will not become part of the wrestler's mental game plan. This is a tool that can give wrestlers a roadmap to success throughout the season. The Wrestling Match Goal Form can help wrestlers become better at setting process and performance goals which in turn can help to develop focus and concentration, relax and control arousal/stress, and ultimately lead to the development of a more confident wrestler.

Coaches must continually encourage wrestlers to be honest in their competitive reflections in order to develop a relationship in which the coach can help the wrestler improve in areas of weakness. The wrestlers should also be assured that their answers are held in confidence for the purpose of improving mental skills. Finally, when using the Wrestling Match Goal Form make sure that the wrestler always list at least two things that went well and two things that didn't go so well. This gives the wrestler and the coach topics from which to build and develop.

Chapter 4

LEG ATTACK DRILLS

Single and double leg attacks have always been deemed effective takedown maneuvers for high school, college, and freestyle wrestlers. Currently, as in the past, they are also premier techniques utilized in international freestyle competition. To be successful with these takedowns, the wrestler must maintain proper stance or position, create motion, lower levels, and penetrate through the opponent. This chapter's drills reinforce four of the seven basic skills: position, motion, level change, and penetration.

These drills are lead-up activities for the development of successful single leg, double leg, high-crotch, and other variations on the leg attack including foot sweeps and ankle picks. Proper stance is important so that the wrestler can defend himself and start an offensive attack of his own.

The stance drills are followed by movement/motion drills. A wrestler who is unable to create motion will find it difficult to score an offensive takedown. The movement drills are designed to teach a wrestler to create an angle on his opponent and effectively attack him. A high percentage of wrestlers who score the first takedown in a match often go on to win the match. Therefore, a wrestler should constantly be moving and on the attack.

The successful leg attack must also include effective changing of levels. Wrestlers must be coached to maintain proper position during the level change. They should bend at the knees and not at the waist; as bending at the waist could result in becoming over-extended and snapped to the mat and taken down by an opponent. The chapter concludes with penetration drills and lead-up activities for foot sweeps and ankle picks.

Effective practice of these drills should increase a wrestler's success rate with the leg attack, whether at the peewee, junior high, senior high, or college level.

CHAPTER INDEX

4.1 Statue Drill

Skill Level: All levels

Basic Skill: Position

Purpose: To assume a proper neutral position wrestling stance

Prerequisite: The wrestlers should have had a proper wrestling stance described and demonstrated for them.

Procedure: The wrestler assumes a proper stance and holds it while you critique him.

Coaching Points: In most stances, the wrestler should have his knees bent, hips square, elbows tight to the body, shoulders and neck rounded forward (like a turtle pulling its head into its shell), and head up. Comment on the stance of each wrestler in the room to assure you've given feedback to all wrestlers and to help everyone feel part of the team.

4.2 Team Mirror Drill

Skill Level: All levels

Basic Skill: Position, motion

Purpose: To create motion while maintaining a proper stance

Prerequisite: The wrestlers must be able to assume a proper neutral position wrestling stance.

Procedure: The wrestlers assume their stances facing the coach. The captain faces the team and begins side-to-side movement. The team mirrors the captain, changing direction as he does. Throughout the motion drill, each wrestler must maintain a proper stance.

Coaching Points: Coaches should demand proper stance throughout this drill.

4.3 Scarecrow Drill

Skill Level: Peewee, junior high

Basic Skill: Position, motion

Purpose: To create motion in front of a stationary opponent

Prerequisite: The wrestlers must be able to assume and maintain a proper neutral position wrestling stance.

Procedure: The dark wrestler stands in a scarecrow position with his arms outstretched to the sides. The light wrestler assumes a proper stance and moves from side to side, first directly in front of his opponent, then in front of one arm, and then back to the other arm *(figure A)*.

Coaching Points: You might advise the offensive wrestler to fake leg attacks in front of each arm during his side-to-side movement. The fakes can be used as a setup for a leg attack.

4.4 Tennis Ball Stance-Maintenance Drill

Skill Level: Peewee, junior high

Basic Skill: Position, motion, level change

Purpose: To keep elbows tight to the body while wrestling from the neutral position

Prerequisite: The wrestler must be able to create motion while maintaining a proper neutral position wrestling stance.

Procedure: Two wrestlers face each other on their feet in proper wrestling stance. One wrestler holds a tennis ball under each armpit. The other wrestler is instructed to destroy the wrestler's stance by using head bangs, push-pulls, and forearm shots. Should the wrestler drop a tennis ball, it is a signal that he has been forced out of the proper position.

Coaching Points: Demonstrate how an opponent may score by using a duck under if the wrestler's elbows are not held tight to the body.

4.5 Tennis Ball Motion Drill

Skill Level: Peewee, junior high

Basic Skill: Position, motion, level change

Purpose: To maintain a proper stance while creating motion, with emphasis on keeping the elbows tight to the body

Prerequisite: The wrestlers must be able to assume a neutral position wrestling stance.

Procedure: The wrestlers are paired and instructed to face each other not more than one arm-length apart. Each wrestler holds a tennis ball in each armpit. One wrestler begins circular motion, changing direction at will. The other wrestler mirrors him, changing direction as he does. Both wrestlers try not to drop the tennis balls.

Coaching Points: Remind wrestlers not to circle so fast that they hop up and down, leaving their legs unprotected.

4.6 Mirror Circle Drill

Skill Level: Peewee, junior high, senior high

Basic Skill: Position, motion

Purpose: To react to an opponent's movement

Prerequisite: The wrestlers should be able to create motion while maintaining a proper stance.

Procedure: The wrestlers are paired and instructed to face each other not more than one arm-length apart. One wrestler begins circular motion, changing direction at will. The other wrestler must attempt to mirror him, changing direction as he does. The roles are reversed in the next session.

Coaching Points: Coaches should caution wrestlers not to circle so fast that they begin to hop up and down. Remind them that they must protect their legs in a match situation and therefore should remain in a low, well-protected stance for this drill.

4.7 Stance-Maintenance Drill

Skill Level: All levels

Basic Skill: Position, motion, level change

Purpose: To react to an opponent's attack by maintaining a proper stance

Prerequisite: The wrestlers must be able to maintain a proper wrestling stance.

Procedure: Wrestlers are paired on their feet, facing each other. One wrestler is assigned to destroy the other wrestler's stance using head bangs, pushes, pulls, forearm shots, and so on. The other wrestler reacts by readjusting his posture to maintain a proper stance. The roles of the wrestlers are reversed in the next session.

Coaching Points: Insist that the offensive wrestler also maintain a proper stance during this drill; remind him that if he uses poor position in practice it may carry over into a match situation.

4.8 Tap Drill

Skill Level: Peewee, junior high, senior high

Basic Skill: Position, motion, level change

Purpose: To be able to lower the level for the purpose of attacking an opponent's legs

Prerequisite: The wrestlers should have been presented with visual and verbal demonstrations of level change methods.

Procedure: The object of this drill is to see how many times a wrestler can tap his opponent's right knee with his right hand in 5 seconds. There are several other similar contests, such as tapping the thigh, calf, ankle, or shoulder. Strategies, such as blocking and penetration, will evolve during this drill.

Coaching Points: Make sure wrestlers understand that they must lower the level by bending at the knees, not at the waist. If a wrestler begins to bend at the waist, allow his opponent to snap him down.

4.9 Sandbag Stance-Maintenance Drill

Skill Level: High school, college

Basic Skills: Position, motion, level change

Purpose: To maintain a neutral position wrestling stance while being attacked

Prerequisite: The wrestlers must be able to remain in a low, standing, neutral position wrestling stance.

Procedure: Wrestlers are assigned to face each other on their feet in a proper wrestling stance. The light wrestler uses head bangs and push-pull movements in an attempt to destroy the dark wrestler's base *(figure A)*. The dark wrestler carries a sandbag as he attempts to maintain his stance; the additional weight helps strengthen the leg muscles while teaching the wrestler to maintain a proper stance while under attack.

Coaching Points: Remind the wrestlers that they must work much harder to maintain position in this drill because they cannot use their arms to block and balance, but instead must rely heavily on their movement and level change for stance maintenance.

4.10 Power Step Penetration Drill

Skill Level: All levels

Basic Skill: Position, motion, level change, penetration

Purpose: To effectively attack an opponent's leg

Prerequisite: The wrestlers should be able to assume a stance, create motion, and change levels.

Procedure: The wrestlers line up in the wrestling room and use the power step for penetration across the length of the mat. A power step is performed by stepping the left toe even with the right heel, lowering the level, and stepping forward with the right foot. In a competitive setting the wrestler would attempt to drive through his opponent or step up and drive across his opponent *(figure A)*.

Coaching Points: Be sure the wrestlers maintain proper position while each penetration step – head up, shoulders over knees, and back straight.

4.11 Leg Lift Penetration Drill

Skill Level: All levels

Basic Skill: Position, motion, level change, penetration

Purpose: To practice penetration skills needed to capture a single leg

Prerequisite: The wrestlers must be able to assume a stance and penetrate.

Procedure: The light wrestler penetrates toward the left leg of the dark wrestler. The dark wrestler lifts his leg as the light wrestler penetrates; this motion allows the light wrestler to penetrate beyond the leg that is to be captured *(figure A)*.

Coaching Points: Remind wrestlers that when they penetrate on an opponent's leg, the leg will usually be moving backward in a sprawl motion, so the penetrating wrestling must penetrate beyond the spot where the leg started.

4.12 Scarecrow Drill for High-Level Penetration

Skill Level: Peewee, junior high

Basic Skill: Position, motion, level change, penetration

Purpose: To create motion and lower the level before penetration

Prerequisite: The wrestlers should have engaged in stance, motion, and level-change drills.

Procedure: The dark wrestler assumes a scarecrow position, with both arms outstretched to the sides. The light wrestler executes a high-level penetration step underneath one of the dark wrestler's arms *(figure A)*. The coach dictates what type of penetration step should be executed.

Coaching Points: Remind the light wrestler that he is penetrating on an imaginary opponent and therefore should visualize the movement in his mind. He should also use the step-up-and-drive movement to finish the drill *(figure B)*.

4.13 T-Shirt Harness Drill

Skill Level: All levels

Basic Skill: Position, motion, level change, penetration

Purpose: To keep elbows tight to the body when penetrating

Prerequisite: Wrestlers must be able to assume a stance, create motion, change levels, and penetrate.

Procedure: The wrestler puts on a t-shirt over his head and down his back into a position even with his elbows. This forces the wrestler's elbows to stay tight to the sides of his body. He faces a partner and begins executing double leg penetration shots *(figure A)*.

Coaching Points: Remind the wrestlers that they should lower levels prior to penetration.

A

4.14 Solo Step-and-Drive Drill

Skill Level: All levels

Basic Skill: Level change, motion, (sub skills – direction change and drive across body)

Purpose: To teach a wrestler how to stand and drive across an opponent's body to finish a takedown attempt

Prerequisite: The wrestlers should have been presented with visual and verbal demonstrations of a step-and-drive finish.

Procedure: The wrestler begins in a one-knee-up, one-knee-down position *(figure A)*. On command, he stands on his left foot and drives across an imaginary opponent *(figure B)*.

Coaching Points: Emphasize that this drill stimulates the action needed to score on a single leg by turning the corner to drive across an opponent's body for a score.

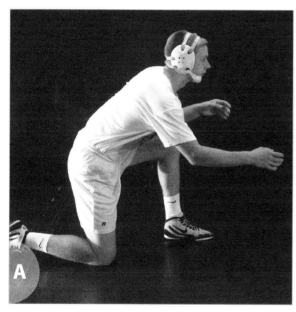

4.15 Knee Change-Turn Corner Drill

Skill Level: Peewee, junior high

Basic Skill: Position, motion, level change, penetration, (sub skill – direction change)

Purpose: To enhance a wrestler's ability to "turn the corner" and create an angle on an opponent when attacking a single leg

Prerequisite: The wrestlers must be able to assume a stance, create motion, change levels, and penetrate.

Procedure:

Shoot-Out (for Primary Wrestlers): The wrestlers line up in two lines facing opposite walls. They are instructed to lower the level and penetrate. They should end up in a position with one knee up and one knee down *(figure A)*. On command, they have a contest to see how fast they can change knees while they pretend to have a gunfight. The hand that would normally go around the leg is holding the imaginary gun *(figure B)*.

Capture (for Intermediate Wrestlers): The light wrestler attacks a single leg with a high crotch and ends up in a knee up—knee down position. The coach may want to play Shoot-out or simply have the light wrestler execute a knee change to capture the leg *(figure C)*.

Capture Fast (for Advanced Wrestlers): The advanced wrestler attacks, executes a knee change and scores a single leg takedown.

Coaching Points: Continually advise wrestlers of the importance of direction change for creating an angle when attacking a single leg. Do not let wrestlers become overextended on their penetration attempts or they will not be able to execute a knee change.

4.16 Drive and Lift Drill

Skill Level: All levels

Basic Skill: Level change, lifting, (sub skills – direction change and drive across)

Purpose: To teach a wrestler to combine direction change with a drive and lift combination in order to finish a single or double leg attack

Prerequisite: The wrestlers must be able to penetrate without becoming overextended.

Procedure: The light wrestler assumes a position on both knees with his right hand up the dark wrestler's crotch and his left arm behind his back. Dark holds light's arm behind his back *(figure A)*. On command, light steps up with his left foot, crosses over into a double leg position with his right arm, and either lifts the dark wrestler or drives him across the mat with his head *(figure B)*.

Coaching Points: Caution the dark wrestler not to raise the light wrestler's captured arm above 90 degrees of flexion at the elbow joint.

Safety Concern: Wrestlers should not wrestle live from this particular position, as injury to the arm might occur.

4.17 Inside Step-Turn Corner Drill

Skill Level: All levels

Basic Skill: Position, motion, level change, penetration (sub skill – direction change)

Purpose: To develop proper penetration and combine that skill with direction change for successful single leg attacks

Prerequisite: The wrestlers must be able to penetrate without becoming overextended.

Procedure: Two wrestlers face each other on their feet not more than one arm-length apart. The offensive wrestler executes a right leg lead penetration step, reaching high into his partner's thigh region. Once penetration has occurred, the defensive wrestler steps in a backward circle motion. Meanwhile, the offensive wrestler brings his left foot up to a position even with his forward foot and changes direction so that he is driving into and across his partner's body. He also uses his arms and changes off to a double leg. This sequence of penetrations and corner turns continues for 30 seconds, and then roles are reversed.

Coaching Points: Reinforce the concept that direction change is very important for a successful leg attack.

4.18 Thrust Drill

Skill Level: Peewee, junior high, senior high

Basic Skill: Position, motion, level change, penetration (sub skill – direction change)

Purpose: To counter a defensive wrestler's whizzer attack

Prerequisite: The wrestlers must be able to rotate at the hips, creating a thrust motion with the elbows.

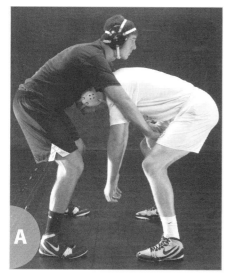

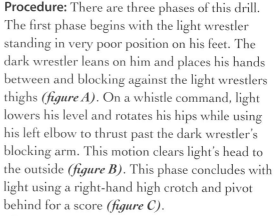

Procedure: There are three phases of this drill. The first phase begins with the light wrestler standing in very poor position on his feet. The dark wrestler leans on him and places his hands between and blocking against the light wrestlers thighs *(figure A)*. On a whistle command, light lowers his level and rotates his hips while using his left elbow to thrust past the dark wrestler's blocking arm. This motion clears light's head to the outside *(figure B)*. This phase concludes with light using a right-hand high crotch and pivot behind for a score *(figure C)*.

The second phase of this drill is to practice the thrust skill when attacking a single leg. The light wrestler locks on a single leg in an overextended position as the dark wrestler counters with a full sprawl and whizzer. The light wrestler steps in on his knees and then thrusts out, using a knee change to finish for the score.

The final phase of this drill is to work the thrust as soon as the defensive partner begins to sprawl in an attempt to counter the single leg attempt.

Coaches Points: Point out that if a wrestler hits a thrust as soon as his opponent whizzers, he will avoid scramble situations down on the mat.

4.19 Front Headlock-Scarecrow Drill

Skill Level: Peewee, junior high, senior high

Basic Skill: Penetration, level change

Purpose: To teach a wrestler to immediately lunge forward, attempting to capture an opponent's leg, when faced with a front headlock situation

Prerequisite: The wrestlers must be able to execute a front headlock or at least understand the principles that make it effective.

Procedure: The dark wrestler assumes a scarecrow position on his knees. The light wrestler begins with his head under one of the dark wrestler's arms *(figure A)*. This simulates a front headlock position. On a whistle command the light wrestler forces his head back and lunges forward on his knees. This motion brings his base underneath his shoulders *(figure B)*. Simultaneously his grabs for an imaginary leg, comes to his feet, and drives across his imaginary opponent.

Coaching Points: Remind your wrestlers that they must not come overextended when put in a front headlock situation. This is a good drill for reinforcing that concept.

4.20 Double-Up Drill

Skill Level: Junior high, senior high

Basic Skill: Position, motion, level change, penetration

Purpose: To correct the offensive wrestler's overextended body position that has resulted from a defensive sprawl

Prerequisite: The offensive wrestlers must be able to penetrate using a double leg maneuver, and the defensive wrestlers must be able to execute a sprawl maneuver.

Procedure: The wrestlers assume positions in which the light wrestler is locked on a double leg with his hands behind the knees of the dark wrestler. The dark wrestler is in a one-half sprawl *(figure A)*. On command, the dark wrestler executes a three-quarter sprawl *(figure B)*. The light wrestler must pull in with his arms and take a step in and up on his knees. This motion should place his hips in an excellent position for a finish *(figure C)*. This routine should be performed for 25 to 30 repetitions in a given time period.

Coaching Points: Use this drill for wrestlers who are fatigued. It will stimulate that 'last shot' often needed to win late in a match.

4.21 Fishhook Snag Drill

Skill Level: Peewee, junior high

Basic Skill: Position, motion, level change, penetration

Purpose: To capture a single leg without putting knees on the mat

Prerequisite: The wrestlers must be able to lower level and penetrate without becoming overextended.

Procedure: The light wrestler fakes a shot on a single leg, then lowers his level and steps his foot toward the dark wrestler. He then pretends that his hands are fishhooks and snags just behind the knee of the dark wrestler. The fishhook action should snag the two cords located on the back of the knee *(figure A)*.

Coaching Points: This is an excellent technique drill for elementary wrestlers. However, remind them they must keep their heads up and looking into the chest of their parteners so that they do not become overextended. Be sure they bend at the knees, not at the waist, when changing levels.

4.22 Leg Pinch Drills

Skill Level: Peewee, junior high

Basic Skill: Position, motion, level change, penetration

Purpose: To control an opponent's leg in a single leg, leg up position without using hands

Prerequisite: The wrestlers must be able to capture a single leg.

Procedure: The light wrestler captures one of the dark wrestler's legs and pinches it between his own. He must control the captured leg without using his hands. He then creates motion and changes levels, all the time controlling the captured leg with his own leg pinch-off *(figure A)*.

Another way to drill this pinch-off is to have races across the mat. One man controls a leg and races across the mat, and then his partner controls his leg for the return trip.

Coaching Points: Have the wrestlers execute a single leg finish at the end of the drill or race. This will simulate and prepare the wrestler for a match situation. Insist that wrestlers maintain a proper stance during this drill.

4.23 Soccer Kick Drill

Skill Level: Junior high, senior high, college

Basic Skill: Position, motion, level change, penetration

Purpose: For the offensive wrestlers, to develop proper timing in order to trip an opponent to the mat; for the defensive wrestlers, to maintain balance in a single leg up situation

Prerequisite: The offensive wrestlers must be able to successfully capture a single leg, and the defensive wrestlers must be able to use a loose whizzer.

Procedure: The light wrestler captures a high single leg and leans back, holding dark's leg. Dark is using a loose whizzer for support as he hops *(figure A)*. The light wrestler attempts to trip dark by kicking dark's shin while he is in the air. The kick should be executed as if attempting to kick a soccer ball. This drill involves a great amount of timing; if the light wrestler doesn't score on the first kick attempt, he should simply try again.

4.24 Knee Block Drill **REVISED**

Skill Level: Junior high, senior high, college

Basic Skill: Position, motion, level change, penetration

Purpose: To develop the rhythm of lifting and blocking in order to score from the neutral position using a foot sweep maneuver

Prerequisite: The wrestlers must be able to assume a double-leg lift position.

Procedure: The offensive wrestler assumes a double-leg lift position. He pivots into the defensive wrestler and pulls him in a circle with his right hand. As the defensive wrestler hops to maintain his balance, the light wrestler uses a knee block for a takedown. This drill helps to teach a wrestler how to set up the sweep by using a circle pull and block.

Coaching Points: Make sure that the wrestlers are merely blocking with their thighs and not using their feet or knees for a tripping motion.

4.25 Foot Sweep Dance

Skill Level: Junior high, senior high

Basic Skill: Position, motion, level change, penetration

Purpose: To develop rhythm for executing a foot sweep

Prerequisite: The wrestlers must be able to assume an inside biceps control situation.

Procedure: The light wrestler hop-steps on his left foot while pulling his partner with his right hand, using his right foot to block the dark wrestler's left shin *(figure A)*. He then hop-steps back on his right foot, pulls with his left hand, and blocks using his left foot. This combination continues for the length of the mat.

Coaching Points: Coaches should stress that the wrestler executing the foot sweep does not need to kick his opponent's shin-only block it with his foot as he pulls. Use this drill after the knee block drill so wrestlers understand the concept of pulling opponent in a circle.

4.26 Heel Pick Drill REVISED

Skill Level: All levels

Basic Skill: Position, motion, level change, penetration

Purpose: To create motion by forcing an opponent to move in a circular pattern

Prerequisite: The wrestlers must be able to control their opponents with a collar tie and wrist control situation.

Procedure: The light wrestler begins in a collar tie and wrist control situation. He circles to his right and then takes a deep circling step back with his left foot, simultaneously pulling with the wrist control hand. This movement causes the dark wrestler's right foot to step toward the light wrestler *(figure A)*. The light wrestler then lowers level, pulling dark's head toward his right knee, and uses his left hand to pick behind dark's right heel *(figure B)*. In a match situation, light would pick the heel and drive the dark wrestler toward his back. In the drill, however, the light wrestler comes back to his feet, circles in the opposite direction, and picks the left heel of the dark wrestler.

Coaching Points: Emphasize how important it is for the wrestler executing the heel pick to attempt to pull the opponent's head toward his knee, thus creating poor position and allowing the successful pick.

4.27 Sparring Drill

Skill Level: Junior high, senior high, college

Basic Skill: Position, motion, level change, penetration (sub skill – direction change, hand control, and drive across)

Purpose: For the offensive wrestlers, to use all of the seven basic skills in executing various takedowns and to recognize various situations that might occur during a match situation; for the defensive wrestlers, to present the offensive man with various match-like situations and to execute a two-on-one hand control stand up immediately following each takedown.

Prerequisite: The wrestlers must be able to execute various takedown maneuvers as well as a stand-up escape.

Procedure: One wrestler executes a setup and a complete takedown. Immediately upon hitting the mat, his partner regains his base and executes a two-on-one hand control stand-up escape. As the wrestlers become more proficient with their takedown maneuvers, the defensive wrestler begins to present various situations for the offensive man to react to.

Coaching Points: This is an excellent way to warm up before actual live competition. It also provides a good cardiovascular workout in any practice setting. As wrestlers improve, insist that they create reaction situations for each other.

4.28 Circle Up Drill **NEW**

Skill Level: All levels

Basic Skill: Position, motion

Purpose: To train wrestlers to keep moving and creating an angle on an opponent when attacking a single leg

Prerequisite: None, except a basic knowledge of a single leg attack.

Procedure: The light wrestler forms a tripod by himself with his hands to simulate locking on a single leg *(figure A)*. He then runs in a circle, simulating the creation of an angle on the opponent. In practicing with a partner, he will run in a circle attempting to turn the corner and finish up on his feet *(figure B)*.

Coaching Points: This is an excellent way to practice creating an angle and getting to one's feet in a single leg attack situation.

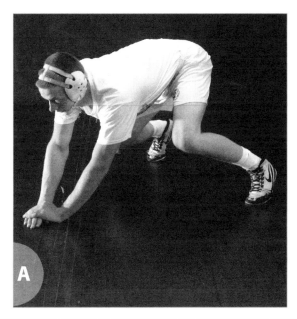

Chapter **5**

UPPER BODY ATTACK DRILLS

The upper body attack is the only attack allowed in Greco-Roman wrestling. However, components of the upper body attack are useful for all phase of wrestling. The basic skills of lifting, back-stepping, and arching are useful for Greco-Roman and Freestyle competitions well as American Folkstyle wrestling.

The drills contained in this chapter serve as lead-up activities for the development of a successful upper body attack, which may include such moves as headlocks, body-locks, saltos, souplesses, and arm throws. As in Chapter 3, the actual techniques are not demonstrated; rather, drills are given that can be used as lead-ups for the upper body maneuvers.

The chapter begins with a demonstration of the proper lifting position needed by a wrestler to lift an opponent from the mat, and the various positions from which lifts may be practiced. Lead-up activities for development of the back arch are followed by back-step drills. The chapter concludes with drills that incorporate the lift, back-step, and back arch into an actual throw. In the throwing drills, a throwing dummy or crash pad is used in an attempt to decrease the possibility of injury.

CHAPTER INDEX

5.1 Lift Drills

Skill Level: Junior high, senior high, college

Basic Skill: Position, motion, level change, lifting, back arch

Purpose: To develop proper lifting position to execute basic lifts during competition

Procedure: Lift drills incorporated into any wrestling practice must emphasize proper lifting position. There are five basic lifts:

Side Lift: The light wrestler uses a side body lock position to lift. The dark wrestler counters with a whizzer *(figure A)*.

Back Lift: The light wrestler locks around the dark wrestler in a rear standing position. The light wrestler performs the lift by stepping between the dark wrestler's legs, lowering levels, and lifting. This is an essential skill because current rules dictate that a rear standing wrestler must return his opponent to the mat quickly *(figure B)*.

Duck Lift: The light wrestler steps in as if to score on a duck under. The dark wrestler attempts a neck wrench. The light wrestler then slips his collar tie hand to the dark wrestler's biceps while moving his free hand to dark's thigh for a proper lifting position *(figure C)*.

High Crotch: Double Leg Lift. This lift incorporates the crossover from a high crotch to a double leg. The light wrestler attempts a high crotch. The dark wrestler defends by pushing light's head to the outside. Light responds by crossing his right hand across dark's waist, lowering levels, and lifting *(figure D)*.

Single Leg Lift: Lifts may also be executed from a single leg position.

Coaching Points: You might wish to have each lift completed with a bring-to-the-mat finish. Many of the lifts can be finished by using some type of the turk or knee block. However, to save practice time you may want only the last of five repetitions completed with some type of bring-to-the mat.

You may also wish to have lifts executed from a fireman's or a bear-hug position. **However, emphasize that in any lift it is mandatory that wrestlers assume proper lifting position:** wrestlers must **(a)** step into opponent while lowering levels, **(b)** keep hips lower than the opponent's, and **(c)** lift using only the legs and a back arch.

5.2 Buddy Squat Drill

Skill Level: Junior high, senior high, college

Basic Skill: Position, level change, penetration

Purpose: To strengthen the quadriceps muscles

Prerequisite: The wrestlers must be able to change levels without the added resistance of partners on their backs.

Procedure: The dark wrestler assumes a neutral position stance. The light wrestler then jumps on dark's back. The light wrestler uses a leg pinch as well as a grip around the dark wrestler's neck to stay on. The dark wrestler should not hold on to the light wrestler's legs; he keeps his hands forward in a stance position. The dark wrestler then does several repetitions of squats as if on a squat rack.

Safety Concerns: Advise your wrestlers that their knees should not be flexed to or beyond 90 degrees. Recent studies have indicated that squatting beyond 90 degrees may harm the knee joint.

5.3 Pummeling Drill

Skill Level: Junior high, senior high, college

Basic Skill: Position, motion, level change

Purpose: To teach wrestlers to keep their elbows tight to their bodies and fight for inside control in an overhook and underhook situations

Prerequisite: The wrestlers must be able to assume an overhook and underhook position.

Procedure: Wrestlers face each other in an overhook and underhook situation *(figure A)*. To pummel, each wrestler takes his overhook hand and forces it down between his opponent's underhook and his own body *(figure B)*, and the wrestlers change head positions from one side to the other *(figure C)*. The wrestlers then perform the routine to the opposite side *(figure D)*. They should begin to keep their arms tight to their sides once they get a feel for the 'swimming' action of the pummel.

Coaching Points: This action simulates a match situation. You may wish to end the drill with one wrestler executing a headlock or body lock. Remind the wrestlers that they must utilize proper wrestling stances and not stand upright.

5.4 Pummel Contest

Skill Level: Junior high, senior high, college

Basic Skill: Position, motion, level change, penetration, lifting, back step, back arch

Purpose: To use pummeling maneuvers to get into position to score during competition

Prerequisite: The wrestlers must be able to execute all of the seven basic skills and have a general knowledge of the basic neutral position scoring maneuvers.

Procedure: The wrestlers begin in an overhook and underhook situation. They pummel until actual competition begins on a whistle command. Points are scored as follows: one point for lifting a man off the mat, two points for getting behind an opponent by using a level-change throw-by, and one point for snapping the opponent forward so that one hand touches the mat. The contest begins with two wrestlers pummeling. They attempt to use a body lock for a lift or a simple arm throw-by for a go-behind score. The snap down maneuver is used only when a wrestler is using his head to block.

Coaching Points: This drill demands that wrestlers maintain good positions while pummeling. If a wrestler leaves his elbows loose, he will be thrown by; if he blocks with his head, he will be snapped down; and if he doesn't maintain good body position, he will be body locked and lifted. This is an excellent Greco-Roman or Freestyle game.

5.5 Wall Backstep Drill **REVISED**

Skill Level: Peewee, junior high, senior high, college

Basic Skill: Position, level change, penetration, back step

Purpose: To introduce the actual steps and develop the rhythm needed to complete the initial portion of a backstep maneuver

Prerequisite: The wrestlers must be able to assume a position and penetrate.

Procedure: The wrestler stands leaning against a wall using his hands for support. His feet are about a foot from the wall. He steps in with his left foot followed by his right foot in a toe-heel position. This step is repeated over and over. Coaches can add part two by having the wrestlers pivot and face the opposite wall completing a backstep.

Coaching Points: Have wrestlers practice this drill to the opposite side using a right-foot lead followed by the left foot to a toe-heel position. Stress that the steps are to be completed very slowly at first, speed increasing with time. This is an excellent drill for a wrestler who is resting during round-robin wrestling. You may wish to provide music for this drill.

5.6 Resistance Band Backstep Drill

Skill Level: Junior high, senior high, college

Basic Skill: Position, level change, penetration, back step

Purpose: To practice the back step maneuver without a partner

Prerequisite: The wrestlers should be able to execute a backstep with a partner.

Procedure: The wrestler first practices the components of a backstep headlock or arm throw using as his partner only elastic bands (an old bicycle inner tube or rubber hose may also be used) tied to a weight machine, a garage door handle, or a set of exercise bars. The wrestler penetrates *(figure A)*, completes a back step, forces his hips through on the imaginary opponent *(figure B)*, and finally pulls the hose in a throwing manner *(figure C)*. Wrestlers can work on this exercise at home, or it can be made part of a circuit training program in the weight room.

Coaching Points: Remind wrestlers to lower levels for each back step and to have the hips lower than the imaginary opponent. Encourage wrestlers to visualize the actual scoring maneuver during each repetition.

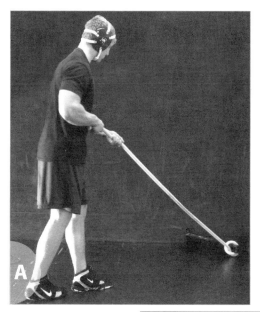

5.7 Hand-Walk the Wall Drill

Skill Level: All levels

Basic Skill: Back arch

Purpose: To be an introductory activity for the back arch

Prerequisite: The wrestlers should be completely warmed up and thoroughly stretched.

Procedure: The wrestler leans backward against a wall, walks down into a back bridge, using only his hands for support, and uses the motor skills needed to perform a back arch *(figure A)*.

Coaching Points: Be sure the wrestlers move into a low squat with the hips moving forward as the upper body goes backward.

Safety Concerns: You may wish to use a spotter for the intitial phase of this drill. This would prevent possible neck injury in case the wrestler's hands slip on the wall.

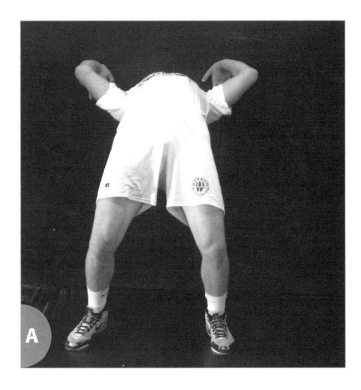

5.8 Rocking Chair Drill

Skill Level: Peewee, junior high, senior high, college

Basic Skill: Motion, back arch

Purpose: To practice the arching motion needed to execute a back arch

Prerequisite: The wrestlers should be able to hand-walk down a wall into a back bridge.

Procedure: This is an individual warm-up drill that begins with the wrestler standing on his knees. He bows his stomach forward, toward the mat, creating a back arch *(figure A)*. A side view of the wrestler makes him appear bent like a bow. The hands are placed near the shoulders. The wrestler falls forward in a rocking-chair motion, using his hands to push over into a back bridge *(figure B, C)*.

Coaching Points: Have all wrestlers loosen and stretch the lower back region before they attempt this drill.

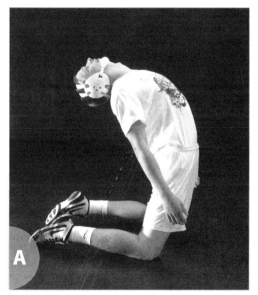

5.9 Hand Grip-Back Arch Drill

Skill Level: All levels

Basic Skill: Back arch

Purpose: To be used as a lead-up activity for executing a back arch

Prerequisite: The wrestlers should be able to Hand-Walk the Wall Drill (Drill 5.7) and execute the Rocking Chair Drill (Drill 5.8).

Procedure: Two wrestlers face each other and grip hands. The light wrestler execute a back arch, while the dark wrestler serves as a safety valve, not allowing the light wrestler to land forcefully on his head as the light wrestler moves to complete the back arch, he must remember to squat, moving his hips forward as he goes backward *(figure A)*. Skill improvement eventually will allow the wrestlers to practice this maneuver using only a single hand grip, and finally to practice the back arch solo.

Coaching Points: Make sure that the partner holding the hands acts as an assistant coach, critiquing each back arch and making suggestions for improvement.

Safety Concerns: Make sure the partner's holding hand is strong enough and does not let the wrestle hit his head on the mat.

5.10 Hip Toss Drill

Skill Level: Junior high, senior high, college

Basic Skill: Penetration, level change, back step, back arch

Purpose: To be used as a warm up for back step

Prerequisite: The wrestlers must be able to execute a back step.

Procedure: The wrestlers lock up in an overhook and underhook situation, the light wrestler uses a right-foot lead back step *(figure A)*. He then pivots his toes and swivels his hips through and under the dark wrestler's waist *(figure B)*. This allows him to lift and toss the dark wrestler over onto his feet *(figure C)*. The dark wrestler then takes his turn and completes a back step hip toss.

Coaching Points: This is an excellent warm-up drill for back stepping because time isn't wasted getting up and off the mat. You might also have your wrestlers use this drill to practice back step headlocks.

5.11 Crash Pad Drills

Skill Level: All levels

Basic Skill: Lifting, back step, back arch

Purpose: To practice throwing maneuvers without the fear of injury

Prerequisite: The wrestlers should understand various throwing maneuvers such as headlocks, body locks, and arching maneuvers.

Procedure: The wrestlers stand near a crash pad and perform throwing maneuvers. Wrestlers may practice headlocks, body locks, saltos, souplesses, and arm throws by throwing their partners onto crash pads.

Coaching Points: Use this drill for wrestlers who have a fear of throwing or being thrown. Allow wrestlers who wish to use the dummy to do so before actually attempting to throw with a live partner.

Note: Coaches can use the high jump mats for this drill. Seek permission from the track coach to use those mats.

5.12 Dummy Drills

Skill Level: Junior high, senior high, college

Basic Skill: Position, motion, level change, penetration, lifting, back step, back arch

Purpose: To practice the basic skills of lifting, back stepping, and throwing without a partner

Prerequisite: The wrestlers must have a basic knowledge of each of the techniques to be performed.

Procedure: The following exercises can be performed using a throwing dummy.

Salto: The wrestler locks around the waist of the dummy and performs a back arch. This belly-to-belly position is known as a salto and can be used only in Freestyle or Greco-Roman competition *(figure A)*.

Souplesse: The wrestler locks around the waist of the dummy from a rear standing position and performs the back arch. This maneuver is also designed only for Freestyle or Greco-Roman competition *(figure B)*.

Arm Throw: The wrestler locks and overhooks on the dummy, does a left-foot lead back step, and finishes with an arm throw *(figure C)*.

Body Lock: The wrestler locks a body lock on the dummy, penetrates, and then takes the dummy to the mat using a back arch *(figure D)*.

Headlock: The wrestler uses head and arm in combination with a back step to take the dummy to the mat *(figure E)*.

Gut Wrenches: The dummy can also be used to practice "gut wrench" maneuvers used to score tilt points in Greco-Roman and Freestyle competition *(figure F)*.

Power Half: The wrestler may practice the power half series on the dummy.

Lift Drills: The dummy can be used for the drills.

Coaching Points: These drills are safe at all levels. The use of a dummy, especially for throwing, allows an inexperienced wrestler to practice the skill without the added fear of injuring a workout partner.

5.13 Slinky Drill

Skill Level: Senior high, college

Basic Skill: Lifting, back arch

Purpose: To practice the back arch using a partner for throwing

Prerequisite: The wrestlers should be able to execute the back arch maneuver using a throwing dummy.

Procedure: The dark wrestler does a handstand facing the light wrestler *(figure A)*. The light wrestler locks around the dark wrestler's waist and begins to execute a back arch *(figure B)*. He should execute the back arch very slowly; as he arches back, the feet of the dark wrestler land on the mat before the light wrestler lands on his head in a bridge position *(figure C)*. The second phase of this drill has the dark wrestler lock around the light wrestler's waist, lift him up and execute the back arch.

Chapter **6**

SETUP, DUCK,
AND DRAG DRILLS

The setup is important for a wrestler's success when wrestling in the neutral position. Setups are essential for consistency at scoring offensive takedowns. Offensive takedowns are usually preceded by some type of action designed to make the opponent react; hand fighting, head fakes, foot fakes, level changes, motion changes, or push-pull actions are typical tactics for "setting up" the opponent.

In some situations an offensive wrestler will use techniques such as an arm drag or duck-under to set up a possible leg attack. The basic skills involved in executing setups are similar to those used in executing most takedowns; stance, motion, level change, and penetration-and the particular skills needed in each situation vary with the type of setup.

This chapter begins with duck-under and arm drag drills, maneuvers that can be used to setup a single or double leg attack. the chapter then presents setups designed to beat the various arm blocks an opponent might present in a match situation, concluding with a setup circuit in which wrestlers travel around the room using appropriate setups for given situations.

Coaches should continually remind wrestlers that setups are integral to the takedown and require perfect practice. In both practice and match situations, wrestlers should be encouraged to use setups before any takedown attempt.

CHAPTER INDEX

6.1 Knee Duck Drill

Skill Level: Peewee, junior high

Basic Skill: Position, penetration (sub skill – direction change)

Purpose: To teach a wrestler the importance of head rotation when attempting to clear an opponent's arm and body using a duck under maneuver

Prerequisite: The wrestlers should have been presented with verbal and visual demonstrations of a complete duck under.

Procedure: The offensive wrestler begins on his knees with his body bent slightly forward. The defensive wrestler drapes his left arm over the head and neck area of the offensive wrestler *(figure A)*. On command, the offensive wrestler steps in on his knees, looks towards the ceiling, and then rotates his head toward the defensive wrestler *(figure B)*. This motion should throw the defensive wrestler's arm off the offensive wrestler.

Coaching Points: Use this drill only as a lead-up activity for the younger kids in the program. Remind the wrestlers to "walk in" to improve their hip position before head rotation.

6.2 Duck Step Drill

Skill Level: Peewee, junior high, senior high, college

Basic Skill: Position, motion, level change, penetration

Purpose: To practice level change and the penetration steps needed to execute a duck under maneuver

Prerequisite: The wrestlers must be able to assume a stance, lower levels, and penetrate.

Procedure: The light wrestler uses double wrist control from the neutral position and executes penetration for a duck under *(figure A)*. He should duck to one side and then to the opposite side during this routine. The actual drill begins with the light wrestler slapping the dark wrestler's hands together, causing the dark wrestler to react by pulling his arms apart. This reaction should create a little space between dark's arm and side for the light wrestler to duck through. The light wrestler lowers level, penetrates with his left foot to the outside, and then ducks under the dark wrestler's arm. He should look immediately to the ceiling; make a quick position check, and then retreat. The duck under penetration step is then executed to the opposite side.

Coaching Points: The same drill may be executed with the dark wrestler using hand control or by having light use a collar-to-biceps combination, or with a double inside-biceps combination.

6.3 Duck Pivot Drill

Skill Level: Peewee, junior high, senior high, college

Basic Skill: Position, motion, level change, penetration (sub skill – direction change)

Purpose: To teach a wrestler to pivot on his toes

Prerequisite: The wrestlers must be able to assume a stance, lower levels, and penetrate.

Procedure: The wrestler assumes a stance resembling a completed duck under penetration step, facing one wall of the wrestling room *(figure A)*. The pivot motion is completed by placing the weight one the toes and rotating to the right facing the front of the room *(figure B)* and finally completing the pivot motion; facing the opposite wall *(figure C)*. The wrestler then pivots back to his original position.

Coaching Points: This is an excellent drill to incorporate with groin stretching exercises. It not only stretches the groin area but also allows for the pivot motion when changing directions.

6.4 No-Hands Duck-Level Change Drill

Skill Level: Peewee, junior high, senior high

Basic Skill: Position, motion, level change, penetration

Purpose: To combine and practice motion, level change, penetration, and the head rotation needed to complete a duck under maneuver

Prerequisite: The wrestlers must be able to perform a basic duck under maneuver.

Procedure: The light wrestler assumes a stance with his hands behind his back, while the dark wrestler gets into a normal square stance. The light wrestler then creates movement, lowers level, and executes a penetration step. He uses only his head to duck under dark's arm, and finishes this portion of the drill by rotating his head toward the dark wrestler *(figure A)*.

Coaching Points: This is an excellent drill for conditioning a wrestler to maintain his stance, creates motion, and score by lowering levels into a head duck. Make sure that wrestlers penetrate by lowering levels at the knees and not by simply bending over at the waist.

A

6.5 Circle Drag Drill

Skill Level: Peewee, junior high, senior high, college

Basic Skill: Position, motion, level change, penetration

Purpose: To counterattack a wrestler who is reaching to block an elbow or shoulder

Prerequisite: The wrestlers should be able to perform an arm drag maneuver.

Procedure: The dark wrestler reaches with his right arm as if he were going to block light's shoulder. The light wrestler moves his left arm in a motion that simulates rotating an airplane propeller in a counterclockwise motion. Light's motion should block the dark wrestler's wrist area *(figure A)*. Light uses his right arm to cup dark's triceps area while lowering levels and penetrating. In a match situation, light might attack a single or double leg or use a leg trip to score. For drill purposes, the dark wrestler steps back attacking with the opposite arm; this allows the light wrestler to practice the circle drag to the opposite side.

Coaching Points: Insist that your wrestlers use an arm drag any time an opponent reaches in an attempt to block their attacks.

6.6 Chop Drag Drill

Skill Level: Peewee, junior high, senior high, college

Basic Skill: Position, motion, level change, penetration

Purpose: To perform an arm drag when the opponent has blocked low on the elbow or chest area

Prerequisite: The wrestlers should be able to perform an arm drag maneuver.

Procedure: The dark wrestler blocks low on the light wrestler's elbow. The light wrestler uses his left hand to chop down on the dark wrestler's wrist *(figure A)*. The chop action clears the opponent's arm, allowing for an offensive arm drag attack *(figure B)*.

Coaching Points: Have your wrestlers practice this setup to both side of the partner's body.

6.7 Blind and Drag Drill

Skill Level: Peewee, junior high, senior high, college

Basic Skill: Position, motion, level change, penetration

Purpose: To obtain a reaction from the opponent by momentarily covering his eyes

Prerequisite: The wrestlers must be able to perform a basic arm drag maneuver.

Procedure: The light wrestler uses his left hand to cover the eye area of the dark wrestler. In most cases the dark wrestler uses his right hand to force the light wrestler's wrist away from his face *(figure A)*. As the dark wrestler pushes the wrist away, the light wrestler uses the motion to reach into dark's armpit area with his right arm and execute an arm drag *(figure B)* while lowering levels, penetrating, and finishing with a right-leg trip *(figure C-D)*.

Coaching Points: Be sure the wrestler lowers level and steps in for the trip as soon as the defensive wrestler begins to clear the hand in front of his eyes.

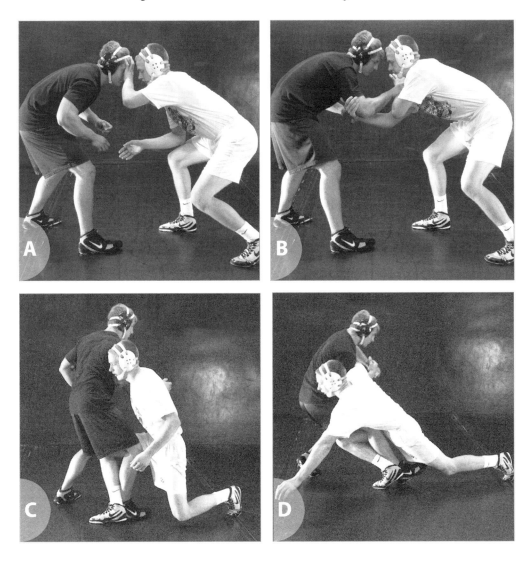

6.8 Movement and Foot Fake Drill

Skill Level: Peewee, junior high, senior high

Basic Skill: Position, motion, level change, penetration

Purpose: To use movement along with fake penetration attempts to set up an opponent for a possible take down

Prerequisite: The wrestlers must be able to assume a stance and create motion.

Procedure: A wrestler moves in his stance while using his lead foot to fake a shot toward his opponent. The object of the foot fake is to cause his opponent to straighten his legs momentarily lock his knees, allowing for a successful leg attack.

Coaching Points: Make sure that your wrestlers are always within one bent-arm's length of their opponents before any foot fake or leg attack. This will help prevent overextension during the actually leg attack.

6.9 Take Control Drill

Skill Level: Peewee, junior high, senior high, college

Basic Skill: Position, motion, level change, penetration

Purpose: To set up a wrestler who will not reach, block or attack and who maintains a good square stance at all times

Prerequisite: The wrestlers must be able to create movement from a proper stance.

Procedure: This drill is similar to the Stance Maintenance Drill. In this situation one wrestler is instructed to maintain a perfect square stance while his partner attempts to move him out of position. The object is to snap, push-pull, and create motion in an attempt to make the opponent reach or step out of position. The offensive wrestler may then lower levels, penetrate, and hopefully score a takedown.

Coaching Points: Insist that the wrestler not forfeit good position while attempting to force his opponent out of position. Acquiring a habit of poor position in practice might allow an opponent to score in a match situation.

6.10 Clear the Arms Drills

Skill Level: Junior high, senior high, college

Basic Skill: Position, motion, level change, penetration

Purpose: To enable a wrestler to identify what type of arm block or tie-up is being used by an opponent and how to effectively score in the various stations

Prerequisite: The wrestlers must be able to create movement from a proper stance.

Procedure: The coach commands one of five movements from the dark defensive wrestler: high shoulder block, low shoulder block, block outside arm, block inside arm, or elbow post. Dark acts, and the light offensive wrestler then uses the proper reaction to clear the block and attack. The following is a list of responses to the given situations.

Beating a High Shoulder Block: The dark wrestler uses a high shoulder block *(figure A)*. The light wrestler forms a V with his left hand, lowers his level, and bumps the dark wrestler's arm off his shoulder (bumping at or above his opponent's elbow). Once the light wrestler has cleared the arm, he is able to attack the dark wrestler's legs.

Beating a Low Shoulder Block: The dark wrestler uses a low shoulder block *(figure B)*. The light wrestler uses a left-hand chop down. Light's outside-in-chop-down motion clears the dark wrestler's arm and enables light to lower levels and penetrate *(figure C)*.

Beating Fingers Outside Arm: When the dark wrestler blocks at the biceps area with his fingers to the outside, the light wrestler reacts with an elbow lift for a high crotch *(figure D)*.

Beating Inside Arm Block: The dark wrestler blocks inside the light wrestler's arm. This action causes the light wrestler to react with a Russian two-on-one *(figure E)*.

Beating an Elbow Post: The dark wrestler uses an elbow post to block the light wrestler. The light wrestler counters with a combination chop and arm drag. This maneuver allows the light wrestler to lower levels and penetrate on the legs of the dark wrestler *(figure F)*.

Coaching Points: You may find that your wrestlers are totally confused when they first practice these skills. If so, practice each block until the responses are mastered. Don't give up; their ability to read and react to situations will improve with practice.

6.11 Reaction Circuit Drill

Skill Level: Junior high, senior high, college

Basic Skill: Position, motion, level change, penetration, back step

Purpose: To teach a wrestler to recognize various situations he may encounter during a match and how he may score against them

Prerequisite: The wrestler should be able to recognize the various situations they will face in this circuit.

Procedure: The coach posts a sign at each station of the circuit indicating the reaction situation for that station. The sign explains the defensive wrestler's action as well as a way to score against that action. The defensive wrestlers stay at that particular station while the offensive wrestlers travel around the circuit. The offensive wrestlers remain at each station for 15 seconds, rotating to the next station on the coach's whistle. After a complete cycle, the offensive wrestlers travel the circuit. The following is a typical reaction setup circuit

Station	Defensive Wrestler's Action	Offensive Wrestler's Reaction
1	Double shoulder block	V the hands and double
2	High shoulder block (1 hand)	V to high crotch or single
3	Low shoulder block (1 hand)	Chop drag to single
4	Reaches toward shoulder	Circle drag to single, double, or trip
5	Grabs both wrists	Clap together to duck under
6	Head tie	Two on one or reverse duck
7	On one or both knees	Snap, shuck, or shrug
8	Force in with underhook	Fireman's or pummel

Coaching Points: This circuit teaches wrestlers how to react to given situations. Encourage the wrestlers to become familiar with the action-reaction signs before actual practice, using mental imagery as they study the signs.

6.12 Aggressive Setup Circuit

Skill Level: Junior high, senior high, college

Basic Skill: Position, motion, level change, penetration, back step, lifting, back arch

Purpose: To practice various setups for takedowns that are designed to be used against a wrestler who maintains a good square stance

Prerequisite: The wrestlers must be able to perform basic setup and takedown maneuvers.

Procedure: The coach posts signs at stations in the wrestling room indicating various setups and particular takedowns to be used with those setups. The wrestlers are divided into two groups, with one group remaining at the stations and assuming square stances. The other group travels the circuit in 15 second intervals, performing the prescribed setups and takedowns. The coach's whistle signals rotation to the next station. Once the first group has completed all of the stations, the groups switch roles.

A setup circuit might include the following activities:

Station	Offensive Setup	Projected Finish
1	Foot fake	Single, double
2	Level change	Single, double, duck, fire
3	Blind and drag	Drag to trip, single or double
4	Collar tie-wrist control	Duck under, single, double
5	Collar tie and motion	Ankle picks
6	Push - pull	Fireman's, single, double, duck
7	Baseball tie	Single, high crotch
8	Underhook	High crotch, ankle pick. Headlock, hip toss, body lock

Coaching Points: Insist that the wrestlers who remain at the stations act as assistant coaches, giving constructive criticism upon completion of each setup and completed takedown. This type of a circuit forces each wrestler to practice all of the setups you've chosen. The individual wrestler will develop one or two favorites, which he will hopefully develop to perfection.

6.13 Adam/The Snap and Shoot
Machine Drill **REVISED**

Skill Level: Peewee, junior high, senior high, college

Basic Skill: Position, motion, level change, penetration, back step, lifting, back arch, stance

Purpose: To practice takedown setups and takedown maneuvers without a partner

Prerequisite: The wrestler should be able to perform basic wrestling maneuvers from the neutral position.

Procedure: A wrestler simply performs takedown setups and takedowns on the Adam takedown machine, which is permanently attached to a wall.

Coaching Points: This machine (Adam) was originally designed 30 years ago by Carl Adams and was updated to the Snap and Shoot Takedown System in 2003. It can be found in many wrestling rooms across the country. This an excellent device for both healthy and injured wrestlers to use during practice.

To order, visit
www.snapandshoot.com
or call 617-783-0328

Photos from Carl Adams

Chapter **7**
NEUTRAL POSITION DEFENSIVE DRILLS

The ability to defend against attack is the final ingredient for success when competing in the neutral position. This chapter focuses on basic lines of defense and counter attacks in the neutral position. The first line of defense is the ability to stop or at least slow an opponent's penetration; these drills involve various head and/or elbow blocks. A second line of defense involves basic hip thrust attempts to free a captured leg. A final line of defense is to free one's legs once the opponent has executed a successful penetration attempt; these drills use sprawl maneuvers to destroy the opponent's base by causing him to become overextended. The object of defense is to stop penetration and begin a counterattack. Drills designed to score on the opponent once his penetration has been slowed and his base has been destroyed include front headlock and hip drag situations.

Finally, wrestlers must have an answer for situations in which the offensive wrestler penetrates so deep that the traditional defenses are rendered ineffective. The final line of defense then will involve the recently-developed "funk" defense. That is the defensive wrestler going over the top of the offensive wrestler and locking around the opponent's waist or in the crotch area in order to prevent a takedown and to begin a counter attack.

A wrestler who practices these drills perfectly should be able to successfully defend himself when competing in the neutral position and effectively counterattack for scores.

CHAPTER INDEX

7.1 Hip Thrust Drill

Skill Level: Junior high, senior high

Basic Skill: Position, motion, level change (sub skill – slow penetration)

Purpose: To teach a wrestler how to use a basic hip thrust to stop or slow an opponent's penetration

Prerequisite: The wrestlers must be able to perform double leg penetration

Procedure: The dark wrestler attempts a half-speed double leg penetration shot. The light wrestler lowers his level and uses his hips to force into the dark wrestler's shoulder area. The thrust action consists of the hips going forward, creating an arch in the back. The dark wrestler then attacks one leg so that the light wrestler can practice using a single hip thrust *(figure A)*.

Coaching Points: Have your wrestlers execute this drill for several repetitions before the Sprawl Drill. It can also be incorporated into the Sprawl Drill (Drill 7.2).

7.2 Sprawl Drill REVISED

Skill Level: All levels

Basic Skill: Position, level change (sub skill–slow penetration, freeing the leg)

Purpose: To teach a wrestler how to free his leg after it has been captured by an opponent.

Prerequisite: The wrestlers must be able to perform single and double leg penetration shots.

Procedure: There are several ways to drill the sprawl. This drill has the following three phases.

Shadow Sprawl: The wrestlers move from side to side in their stances. The coach feints a shot toward the group. The wrestlers immediately sprawl back, dropping to the mat. (The wrestlers should be advised to drop one hip more than the other, to stimulate defending against a single leg shot.) Wrestlers should circle once they get to their feet.

No-Hands Sprawl: The phase involves using a partner, who makes an actual leg attack. The dark wrestler shoots a single, and the light wrestler sprawls using only his hips (no hands) to counter *(figure A)*. The hip of the leg being attacked is dropped much lower than the other hip.

Full Contact Sprawl: The dark wrestler attacks a single or double leg. The light wrestler sprawls with a whizzer and a head push-away *(figure B)*.

Coaching Points: You may want to start by exposing your wrestlers to the Hip Thrust Drill (Drill 7.1) before beginning this drill. The Give Ground Drill (Drill 7.3) is a very beneficial exercise for the wrestler to learn next. **In all instances wrestlers should be reminded to circle once they come back to their feet so not to give the opponent a stationary target to attack.**

7.3 Give Ground Drill

Skill Level: Junior high, senior high, college

Basic Skill: motion, level change (sub skill – freeing the leg)

Purpose: To teach a wrestler to give ground instead of giving up a takedown when defending himself in the neutral position

Prerequisite: The wrestlers should be able to execute single and double leg takedown maneuvers and have a general knowledge of the sprawl defense.

Procedure: Wrestlers are paired facing each other on their feet. One wrestler attacks a double leg and continues to drive through his partner. The light wrestler sprawls *(figure A)* until dark walks him into a near-standing position. At this point, light must give ground or be taken down. Giving ground simply means that he must throw his legs in a backward motion *(figure B)*. This movement pattern continues across the length of the mat; dark walks in and up on a double leg attack, light gives ground, and so on. Once the wrestlers near the opposite wall, the coach instructs the light wrestler to score using a hip drag or front headlock counterattack.

Coaching Points: Make sure your wrestlers realize the importance of giving ground. Before completing this drill, you may want the man using the double leg to score, thus demonstrating why ground must be given.

7.4 Tennis Ball Sprawl Drill

Skill Level: Peewee, junior high

Basic Skill: Position, motion, level change (sub skill – freeing the leg)

Purpose: To improve movement time in the sprawl

Prerequisite: The wrestlers must be able to assume a neutral position wrestling stance.

Procedure: This drill begins with each wrestler holding a tennis ball under each armpit and assuming a neutral position wrestling stance. On a whistle command, the wrestlers drop the balls and attempt to sprawl in a back-and-downward motion to the mat before the balls hit the mat.

Coaching Points: This drill is excellent for breaking the monotony of the daily routine. However, this drill is time consuming and the wrestlers will eventually become bored, so it should only be used once or twice per season.

7.5 Snap Down Drill

Skill Level: All levels

Basic Skill: Position, motion, level change (sub skill – slow penetration, counterattack)

Purpose: To learn to change levels and destroy an opponent's penetration attempt with an elbow block and then score using a snap down maneuver

Prerequisite: The wrestlers should have been presented with verbal and visual presentations of the entire snap down maneuver.

Procedure: The dark wrestler is up-right on his knees, leaning slightly forward. The light wrestler will perform the snap downs. He delivers a blow with his left forearm to dark's right collarbone area; his right hand (thumb down) blocks dark in the shoulder – armpit area *(figure A)*. This motion helps to destroy or slow an opponent's penetration. Once the block has been delivered, the light lets both hands slide past dark's head and shoulder *(figure B)*. The snap down portion of this drill is completed by having light cup his hands behind dark's head and armpit, snapping in a downward and to-the-side motion. This motion should allow the light wrestler to spin to the opposite side for a score *(figure C)*.

Coaching Points: This drill could also be expanded to include snaps and shrugs to either side. Snap-shrugs are accomplished by directing the head in the direction opposite to the spin. This drill can also be incorporated with the Snap Down Spin Drill (Drill 8.6).

7.6 Shoot the Airplane Drill

Skill Level: Peewee, junior high, senior high

Basic Skill: Position, motion, level change (sub skill – counterattack)

Purpose: To counter the double leg attack of an opponent who penetrates with his elbows away from his body

Prerequisite: The wrestlers must be able to execute double leg penetration.

Procedure: The offensive wrestler attempts a double leg penetration shot with his arms out to the side much like airplane wings. As the offensive wrestler penetrates, the defensive wrestler lowers his level and stops the momentum with an overhook–underhook combination *(figure A)*. The light wrestler pancakes the dark wrestler to his back *(figure B)*.

Coaching Points: Peewee wrestlers may want to make airplane noises upon penetration, complete with crash and burn sounds as they go to their backs. In fact, many varsity wrestlers will enjoy making the same sounds.

7.7 Front Headlock/ Throw-by Drill

Skill Level: Junior high, senior high, college

Basic Skill: Motion
(sub skill – counterattack)

Purpose: To overextend an opponent, create motion after capturing a front headlock, and react to the opponent's movements

Prerequisite: The wrestlers must be able to apply the front headlock maneuver.

Procedure: The light wrestler captures a front headlock off a failed shot from the dark wrestler, then immediately overextends the dark wrestler and begins circling to the left. How he scores depends on the dark wrestler's reaction. If dark attempts to force to the inside of the elbow that is over his head, then light throws him to the left *(figure A)*. If dark attempts to force that elbow to the outside, light stops and throws dark's head and arm in the opposite direction (to the right) *(figure B)*.

Coaching Points: Be sure the wrestlers overextend their partners before they begin to circle and create motion. In a match situation, an opponent may be able to walk-in on his knees and capture a leg if he is not overextended. You may wish to add a thigh block to this drill once the throw-bys are mastered *(figure C)*.

7.8 Hip Drag/High Leg Drill

Skill Level: Junior high, senior high, college

Basic Skill: Position, motion (sub skills – freeing the leg, counterattack)

Purpose: To use direction chance in defending against a single leg

Prerequisite: The wrestlers must be able to perform a high-leg over and hip drag maneuvers.

Procedure: The dark wrestler locks onto one leg of the light wrestler. Dark is overextended to simulate a poor shot and an effective sprawl by the light wrestler. In the first phase of this drill, light uses his right hand to reach over the top of dark's neck and grab his right armpit. Light's left hand reaches into the crotch area. Light attempts to pull himself around behind dark using the right-hand arm drag and the left-hand crotch pull and uses a right-leg high-leg over to try to break the dark wrestler's grip *(figure A)*. In the second phase of this drill the light wrestler uses a left-leg high-leg over to break the dark wrestler's grip on his leg *(figure B)*. He then spins to the opposite side for a score. The left-leg high leg would be used only after the right-leg high left has failed. This drill is conducted continuously for 30 seconds, using a hip drag to one side and a high lift to the opposite side.

Coaching Points: Make sure each wrestler reaches over the top for his partner's head and not under his neck. If a wrestler reaches under the neck in an attempt to hip drag his opponent, he will be setting himself up for a sucker drag.

7.9 Hip Drag the Table Drill

Skill Level: Peewee, junior high, senior high

Basic Skill: Motion (sub skills – counterattack)

Purpose: To use a hip drag for a defensive score

Prerequisite: The wrestlers must be able to perform a hip drag maneuver.

Procedure: One wrestler attempts to maintain a tabletop position (down referee's position) and may circle only to avoid being scored upon. The top man executes as many hip drags as possible in a given time period. The roles are then reversed. The winner is the one who scores the most times.

Coaching Points: Remind the bottom man that he may not use his hands to prevent being scored upon.

7.10 Whizzer Drill-Down

Skill Level: Peewee, junior high, senior high, college

Basic Skill: Position, motion, level change (sub skill – freeing the leg)

Purpose: To give the defensive wrestler another weapon to prevent his opponent from attacking and successfully scoring on a leg attack

Prerequisite: The wrestlers should have been presented with visual and verbal demonstrations of the whizzer maneuvers.

Procedure: The light wrestler assumes a position on all fours. The dark wrestler hooks light's left leg and places his right arm across his back. The light wrestler then makes a windmill action with his left arm, attaining a whizzer position *(figure A)*. This alignment now becomes a scrimmage situation. Light attempts to hip into dark while straightening his captured leg *(figure B)*. He must then sit the captured leg to the front *(figure C)* and face his opponent. The dark wrestler meanwhile attempts to keep the leg hooked. Coaches may wish to allow the light wrestler to execute a pancake as he squares to the front.

Coaching Points: You may wish to allow the dark wrestler to use whizzer counters such as a limp arm or an alligator roll-through to score the actual takedown.

7.11 Whizzer Drill-Up NEW

Skill Level: Peewee, junior high, senior high, college

Basic Skill: Position, motion, level change (sub skill–freeing the leg)

Purpose: To give the defensive wrestler another weapon to prevent his opponent from attacking and successfully scoring on a leg attack once the opponent is up on his feet

Prerequisite: The wrestlers should have been presented with visual and verbal demonstrations of the whizzer maneuvers.

Procedure: The dark wrestler holds light's leg in a single leg position. The light wrestler maintains a light whizzer position with his left arm and holds the wrist of the offensive wrestler *(figure A)*. This alignment now becomes a scrimmage situation. Light attempts to hop and maintain balance while attempting to break the dark wrestler's grip on his leg by pulling up with the arms and shooting the captured leg down and backward *(figure B)*. The light wrestler attempts to maintain balance until the grip can be broken.

Coaching Points: This is a last resort position for the light wrestler and he needs to understand that he must maintain his balance by hopping or getting heavy if he gets lifted.

7.12 Defensive Circuit Drill REVISED

Skill Level: Junior high, senior high, college

Basic Skill: Position, motion, level change, penetration, back step, lifting, back arch
(sub skills – slow penetration, freeing the leg, counterattack)

Purpose: To recognize various attacks that may be used in a match situation and how to properly defend against them

Prerequisite: The wrestlers must be able to recognize the attacks to be used in the circuit and how to effectively defend against them.

Procedure: This circuit is similar to the Aggressive Setup Circuit (Drill 6.12) in that half the wrestlers stay at particular stations while the rest travel from station to station. After a complete circuit, the two groups exchange roles.

Station	Offensive Action (Stationary Group)	Defensive Reaction (Traveling Group)
1	Single leg shot	Sprawl, hip drag
2	Double leg shot	Snap down and spin
3	On mat, leg hooked, arm across back	Whizzer counter and pancake
4	Single leg up captured	Pull up to clear or force head outside and kick over cradle
5	Headlock	Step to front and throw
6	Body lock attempt	Metzgar
7	Ankle pick	Shuck by
8	Whizzer	Whizzer counter (limp arm, etc.)
9	Double leg (in deep)	Come over top, lock on waist or crotch and "funk"

Coaching Points: The stationary man should act as an assistant coach, giving constructive criticism on each wrestler's reaction at his station. You may alter the circuit drill to meet your team's needs.

7.13 Funk Drill **NEW**

Skill Level: Peewee, junior high, senior high, college

Purpose: To give the defensive wrestler a weapon to prevent his opponent from successfully scoring on a leg attack once the attack has passed initial defenses.

Prerequisite: The wrestlers should have been taught basic funk maneuvers.

Procedure: The dark wrestler assumes a deep double leg position. The light wrestler reaches across dark's back and locks in the crotch *(figure A)* or around the waist *(figure B)*.

Coaching Points: Coaches may want to practice the skills to score from this position prior to engaging in this drill (for more funk positions see Chapter 12 page 261).

7.14 Attack-Counterattack Drill REVISED (Traditional defense)

Skill Level: Peewee, junior high, senior high, college

Basic Skill: Position, motion, level change, slow penetration (sub skills – freeing the leg, counterattack)

Purpose: To begin a counterattack immediately after an opponent's penetration has been stopped

Prerequisite: The wrestlers should have a basic knowledge of both offensive and defensive scoring maneuvers.

Procedure: The offensive wrestler attempts a double leg attack. The defensive wrestler stops the penetration with an elbow block—snap combination. As the offensive begins to return to his neutral stance, the defensive wrestler transitions to offense wrestler and is instructed to attack using his own double or single leg shot.

Coaching Points: A wrestler has many opportunities in a match situation in which he may be able to score immediately following his opponent's failed attack. This drill helps accustom wrestlers to this fact.

7.15 Attack-Counterattack Drill NEW (From the funk)

Skill Level: Peewee, junior high, senior high, college

Purpose: To begin a counterattack immediately after an opponent's penetration has beaten traditional defenses.

Prerequisite: The wrestlers should have a basic knowledge of both scoring maneuvers in the funk position.

Procedure: The offensive wrestler attempts a double leg attack and penetrates deep on the defensive wrestler's leg. The defensive wrestler immediately goes over the top and locks in the crotch or around the waist of the offensive wrestler. The "funk" man is now on the offensive (See pictures in Chapter 12 on page 261).

Coaching Points: A wrestler has many opportunities in a match situation in which he may be able to score immediately following his opponent's failed attack. This drill helps accustom wrestlers to this fact.

7.16 The Takedown Defender Machine Drills **NEW**

Skill Level: Peewee, junior high, senior high, college

Purpose: To practice defensive (e.g., defensive sprawl, snap and spin, arm drag and spin, front headlock, and proper set point for the feet position) maneuvers without an actual partner

Prerequisite: The wrestlers should be able to perform basic defensive wrestling maneuvers from the neutral position

Procedure: A coach or partner pushes the machine toward the defensive wrestler where he executes a pre-determined defensive maneuver.

Coaching Points: This machine (Takedown Defender) was originally designed by Carl Adams in 2006. It is growing in popularity and can increasingly be found in wrestling rooms across the country. This an excellent device for both healthy and injured wrestlers to use during practice.

To order, visit
www.snapandshoot.com
or call 617-783-0328

Photo with permission from Snapandshoot.com

Chapter **8**

TOP MAN DRILLS

In collegiate, Freestyle, and Greco-Roman wrestling, total time spent wrestling from the advantage position has declined over time. Freestyle and Greco-Roman rules still limit the time that may be spent in the advantage position without scoring points. When this book was last written folkstyle wrestling, college and high school wrestlers had become more than willing to play the two-for-one takedown game, working for bonus decisions rather than for the actual fall. In today's matches, wrestlers have become more efficient from the advantage position to score near fall points with tilts. And, pinning is still the name of the game! It is indeed the talented, dominant grappler who can ride an opponent and eventually turn them to their back and force them into the submission of a pin.

A basic skill section *will not* be included in this chapter for Top Man Drills. The basic skills needed for advantage wrestling are not clearly defined but might center on the ability of the top man to destroy the bottom man's base by continually controlling his hip movement and his hip position. Also, in recent years the impact of Freestyle wrestling is seen in the ability of wrestlers to tilt their opponent for "cheap tilt" near-fall points.

This chapter includes riding drills, such as spinning and floating (reaction) drills, and pinning drills, such as cradle and leg drills. There are also several contests that stress the tilting of an opponent.

This chapter's drills will help improve the top man's ability to ride, turn for back points, and finally (hopefully) pin an opponent.

CHAPTER INDEX

8.1 Basic Spin Drill

Skill Level: All levels

Purpose: To enhance the top man's ability to move around an opponent

Prerequisite: None

Procedure: This drill promotes swift mobility for the offensive wrestler while creating an awareness of points of attack from the top position. The drill begins with wrestlers in an up-down referee's position. On a whistle command, the light wrestler begins to spin around the dark wrestler. Light's chest is positioned on the small of dark's back. While the light wrestler spins, he attacks various body parts of the defensive wrestler *(figure A)*. For instance, when he circles around dark's head, he may push the head down or attack under an armpit. He can also attack under an arm and pick an ankle when at the side, or use a double underhook from the back.

Coaching Points: Make your wrestlers aware of which body parts might be attacked during the spinning motion.

8.2 Back-to-Back Spin Drill

Skill Level: Peewee, junior high, senior high, college

Purpose: To enhance a wrestler's balance while using a high-leg over maneuver during the spin drill

Prerequisite: Wrestlers must be able to perform a high-leg maneuver.

Procedure: This drill is performed in the same manner as the Basic Spin Drill (Drill 8.1), except that light does not attack dark's body parts. Instead, light begins to spin around in a chest-on-back position. He executes a high-leg over maneuver, which brings him into a back-to-back position *(figure A)*. Light continues to spin and does another high-leg over into a chest-on-back position. The light wrestler may not use his hands for this drill, as it is a balance drill.

Coaching Points: Make sure your wrestlers practice the high-leg over maneuvers before attempting this drill.

8.3 Reaction Spin Drill

Skill Level: Peewee, junior high, senior high, college

Purpose: To allow the top man to react to a given situation while spinning

Prerequisite: Wrestlers should be able to spin around an opponent.

Procedure: The Basic Spin Drill (Drill 8.1) is expanded here to include reaction. The coach may choose to blow a whistle indicating that the light wrestler should reverse the direction of his spin. The dark (down) wrestler raises an arm to prevent the light wrestler from spinning around *(figure A)*. Immediately, the light wrestler must react by changing directions and spinning in the opposite direction for a simulated score.

Coaching Points: You might want to use a whistle command for direction change at the beginning of the drill. For a more realistic situation, encourage the down man to lift an arm to stop the spin-around, forcing the top man to spin in the opposite direction.

8.4 Cradle Reaction Spin Drill **NEW**

Skill Level: Peewee, junior high, senior high, college

Purpose: To allow the top man to recognize an opportunity capture a near-side or far-side cradle during the spin drill

Prerequisite: Wrestlers should be able to spin around an opponent.

Procedure: The Basic Spin Drill (Drill 8.1) is expanded here to include the capturing of a cradle lock. The coach may choose to blow a whistle indicating that the dark wrestler should raise one knee toward his own head *(figure A)*. The light (top) wrestler then captures a near-side or far-side cradle. Once captured, the top man releases and continues to spin in the opposite direction.

Coaching Points: You might want to use a whistle command for direction change at the beginning of the drill. For a more realistic situation, encourage the down man to lift an arm to stop the spin-around, forcing the top man to spin in the opposite direction.

8.5 Live Spin Drill

Skill Level: Peewee, junior high, senior high, college

Purpose: To engage in scramble wrestling situations

Prerequisite: The wrestlers should be able to perform the Basic Spin Drill (Drill 8.1) and have a basic knowledge of top and bottom man maneuvers.

Procedure: The entire series of spin drills may be expanded to include live wrestling. Near the end of a spin drill, the coach blows a whistle indicating that the wrestlers should wrestle live. This provides scramble-situation wrestling.

Coaching Points: You might want to use this drill as a contest to see whether the bottom man can score an escape or a reversal.

8.6 Snap Down Spin Drill

Skill Level: Peewee, junior high, senior high, college

Purpose: To combine the Basic Spin Drill (Drill 8.1) with the Snap Down Drill

Prerequisite: The wrestlers must be able to perform the Basic Spin Drill

Procedure: The wrestlers face each other with one wrestler on his knees and the other in a neutral position wrestling stance. Upon command the standing wrestler executes a snap down–spin-around maneuver.

Coaching Points: Constantly remind your wrestlers to look for a spin-around immediately following any snapdown maneuver.

8.7 Floating Drill

Skill Level: Peewee, junior high, senior high, college

Purpose: To allow the top man to react to the bottom man's movements

Prerequisite: The wrestlers should be able to perform basic top and bottom man maneuvers.

Procedure: The offensive wrestler begins on top in a chest-on-back position with his hands under the down wrestler's armpits. The bottom man completes a series of moves as the top man reacts. The moves and countermoves involved in a short series might include switch-reswitch, roll-reroll, sit-out-spin behind, sit-out-drag around, stand-up - back-heel trip, and Granby–log roll.

Coaching Points: Make up any routine you wish. But be sure to encourage the wrestlers to move at full speed, both when acting and when reacting. This will insure full speed transfer into a match situation.

8.8 Ride at All Cost Contest

Skill Level: Junior high, senior high

Purpose: To practice maintaining control of an opponent by utilizing counter maneuvers rather than breaking him flat on the mat.

Prerequisite: The wrestlers must be able to execute basic bottom man maneuvers and their counters.

Procedure: The bottom man is assigned to use any moves except for a stand-up to score an escape or reversal. The top man is told to ride the bottom man using only counters to his moves; he is not allowed to score breakdowns. These combinations might include the switch-reswitch, roll-reroll, sit-out-spin around, and Granby–log roll.

Coaching Points: This is a live wrestling situation, and again you should give some type of reward to assure maximum effort.

8.9 Frog in – Bump down Drill

Skill Level: Peewee, junior high

Purpose: To increase the top man's ability to destroy the bottom man's base immediately following a whistle start

Prerequisite: The wrestlers must be able to assume an up–down referee's position.

Procedure: The wrestlers assume an up–down referee's position. The top man is told to pretend he is a frog. He uses his legs to drive into the bottom man much as a frog would to leap *(figure A)*. The top man may use his arms to block under an arm on the near side and under the thigh on the far side. On a whistle command, the top man leaps into the bottom man and knocks him off of his base.

Coaching Points: Be sure your wrestlers understand that it is very important to destroy the bottom man's base as soon as the whistle blows. It might be advisable to make this a 10-second whistle drill.

8.10 Ride the Barrel Contest

Skill Level: Junior high, senior high

Purpose: To allow the top man to maintain control without destroying the bottom wrestler's base

Prerequisite: The wrestlers must be able to perform rolls and elevators.

Procedure: The wrestlers begin with the dark wrestler in the down referee's position and the light wrestler on top with his arms around dark's waist but not locked *(figure A)*. The object of this contest is for the bottom man to attempt to pull the top man into a position where his hip, buttocks, or shoulders touch the mat. Each time one of these body parts touches the mat, a point is scored. The bottom man may use rolls or elevators to score, while the top man counters using only rotation and a leg post. The top man may deduct a point from the bottom man's score if he can successfully re-roll and remains in a parallel position. However, in this situation, should the bottom man get perpendicular during the re-roll, he (the bottom man) scores a point. The roles are reversed for the next timed session.

Coaching Points: Give some type of reward for the winner, or the wrestlers may not keep true scores.

8.11 Calf Roping Drill

Skill Level: Junior high, senior high

Purpose: To utilize skills needed for tilting an opponent from the two-on-one near-arm chop position

Prerequisite: The wrestlers must be able to perform a two-on-one near-arm tilt.

Procedure: One wrestler is the calf and attempts to run on his hands and knees the length of the wrestling room without being tilted. The other wrestler is the cowboy; he starts in a hover position over the calf *(figure A)*. As the contest begins, the cowboy attempts to do a near-arm chop with a two-on-one tilt. The cowboy is not allowed to tackle the calf—he must hover and use the near-arm chop *(figure B)*.

Safety Tips: This drill is relatively safe, but do not allow the top man to use a tackle for a breakdown.

8.12 Steer Wrestling Contest

Skill Level: Peewee, junior high, senior high

Purpose: To utilize skills needed to perform a spiral ride

Prerequisite: The wrestlers must be able to perform a spiral ride

Procedure: One wrestler starts on his hands and knees as the bull. The other wrestler starts in a hover position with one underhook in place *(figure A)*. The object is for the bull to run the length of the room on his hands and knees without being turned toward one of the side walls. The top man uses his underhook arm to run a spiral and force the bottom man to face a side wall *(figure B)*. The top man must run toward the bottom man's head to turn him toward a wall, just as he would have to do to break down an opponent for a spiral ride.

Coaching Points: This contest will provide a welcome relief from the normal daily routine of practice. Remind the top man to always run toward the head when attempting to score a breakdown using a spiral.

8.13 Cradle Floating Drill

Skill Level: Peewee, junior high, senior high

Purpose: To create an awareness of the opportunities available for the top man to apply a near or far side cradle

Prerequisite: The wrestlers must be able to perform near-and far-side cradle maneuvers

Procedure: This drill is similar to the Floating Drill, except the top man is continually attempting to lock up a cradle. The defensive wrestler does a series of sit-outs and/or starts numerous stand-ups. The offensive wrestler rides from the back in a chest-on-back position with hands underneath the defensive dark wrestler's armpits. Each time the bottom (defensive) wrestler lifts a knee close to his head, the top (offensive) man spins to that side and captures a cradle.

Coaching Points: You must teach your wrestlers the top man phrase "head to knee – that's for me." Each time the bottom man puts his head near his knee, have the top man sing the phrase as he captures a cradle.

8.14 Cradle Confidence Drill

Skill Level: Peewee, junior high, senior high

Purpose: To develop confidence for using the near-side cradle

Prerequisite: The wrestlers must be able to apply a near-side cradle.

Procedure: Two wrestlers lock near-side cradles on each other and begin to roll around on the mat *(figure A)*. They are allowed to roll for 15 to 30 seconds. The coach then signals for live wrestling to commence and roll around the mat *(figure B)*. The wrestler who is on top must release his cradle immediately and flatten on top of the defensive wrestler so he will not be rolled to his back.

Coaching Points: Wrestlers who are caught on the bottom when the live wrestling whistle blows should be instructed not to panic. In many cases the will be able to arch and roll the opponent to his back.

8.15 Jump and Half Nelson Drill

Skill Level: Peewee, junior high, senior high

Purpose: To teach the top man to jump and shoot a half nelson when his opponent has lifted an arm from the mat

Prerequisite: The wrestlers must be able to apply a half nelson.

Procedure: The bottom man (dark) lies flat on the mat with the light wrestler covering him. The dark wrestler uses his right hand to push back into the light wrestler to regain his base *(figure A)*. The light wrestler, immediately upon seeing an opening for a half nelson, jumps to that side and forces dark's arm up with an elbow-on-elbow position *(figure B)*. In a match situation the light wrestler would use a half nelson to work for the fall, but for drill purposes dark reacts by balling in the opposite direction. This movement causes light to jump to the opposite side and catch dark's elbow with his own elbow. The half nelson would follow.

Coaching Points: This drill teaches the bottom man to react to pressure, at the same time allowing the top man to look for openings to shoot a half nelson. Insist that the top man use his elbow to lift the down man's elbow up in the air before putting in a half nelson.

8.16 Bear Crawl to the Head NEW

Skill Level: Peewee, junior high, senior high

Purpose: To teach the top man to crowd toward an opponent's head searching for an opportunity to secure a half nelson from a cross body scramble position

Prerequisite: The wrestlers must be able to apply a half nelson.

Procedure: The bottom man (dark) lies in a belly-up crab position *(figure A)* with the light wrestler covering him in a belly down crab position. On command, the light wrestler attempts to crowd toward the dark wrestler's upper body-head to secure a half nelson. The dark wrestler attempts to race backwards as to avoid being crowed to his back. Ultimately the light wrestler will secure a half nelson finish.

Coaching Points: This drill teaches the top man to crowd into an opponent in an attempt to secure a half nelson and back points.

8.17 Crossface Cradle and Turk Drill

Skill Level: Junior high, senior high, college

Purpose: To teach the top man to react with a crossface cradle or turk for a near fall depending upon the bottom man's reaction

Prerequisite: The wrestler's must be able to perform a crossface cradle and a turk maneuver.

Procedure: The dark wrestler is broken down into a position flat on the mat. The light wrestler then applies a crossface with his left hand and a block behind the knee with his right hand in an attempt to apply a crossface cradle *(figure A)*. The bottom man meanwhile reacts to the pressure by turning into the top man. This causes the top man to release the knee block and pick up the near knee with his right hand *(figure B)*. The light wrestler then steps in and scores with a turk *(figure C)*. For drilling purposes only, the light wrestler then releases the turk, allowing the dark wrestler to turn away. The reaction by the dark wrestler causes the light wrestler to apply and score with a crossface cradle *(figure D)*.

Coaching Points: Make your wrestlers aware that whichever direction the bottom man turns, the top man should be able to score back points.

8.18 Lift or Screw Drill

Skill Level: Junior high, senior high, college

Purpose: To return a man to the mat from the rear standing position

Prerequisite: The wrestlers must be able to perform basic lifts and the screw down maneuver

Procedure: This drill is a contest to see how many times the light wrestler can either lift the dark wrestler off the mat or screw him down into a takedown position. The rear standing man scores a point each time he completes a successful lift or takedown using the screw down maneuver *(figure A)*. The winner of this contest is the wrestler who scores the most points in a given time period. The screw down is completed from the rear standing position by putting pressure on the quadriceps muscles with one's elbow. The bottom man must go down to a position where at least one knee is on the mat.

Coaching Points: In today's wrestling, the top man must be taught to bring the bottom man to the mat immediately; otherwise he may be penalized for stalling. If there are no takedowns or lifts scored in a 30-second time period, you might wish to penalize the top man one point.

8.19 Standing Ride Contest

Skill Level: Peewee, junior high, senior high

Purpose: To maintain control of a wrestler from the rear standing position without locking hands

Prerequisite: The wrestlers should have basic knowledge of the hand control concept.

Procedure: The wrestlers assume a stand-up–rear standing position. The top man is not allowed to lock his hands but must attempt to maintain control for a certain time period. The bottom man attempts to score escapes using hand control. Roles are reversed for the next time period. The winner is the one who scores the most escapes.

Coaching Points: This is a good drill to simulate the final seconds of a match. The top man must maintain control to win.

8.20 Half Nelson Cross Drill **REVISED**

Skill Level: Peewee, junior high, senior high, college

Purpose: To teach wrestlers how to fight off their backs and avoid being pinned

Prerequisite: Each wrestler must be able to perform a back bridge with an opponent on his chest

Procedure: The bottom wrestler lies flat on his back with the top wrestler lying perpendicularly across his chest. The two bodies form a cross. In a live situation, the top wrestler begins with a light half nelson and crotch combinations and the bottom wrestler bridges and attempts to clear an arm and get belly-down. Prior to completing this in combat, the wrestlers should be shown in a passive situation how to bridge and clear an arm between their bodies in defense of a half nelson.

Coaching Points: Be sure your wrestlers understand that to fight off one's back, one must get an arm through between oneself and the opponent's body. Many wrestlers attempt to turn belly-down, but they cannot because their opponents keep them down by blocking the arm.

8.21 Leg-Hip Action Drill

Skill Level: Peewee, junior high

Purpose: To teach wrestlers proper hip and back positions when attempting to use legs

Prerequisite: None

Procedure: A wrestler lies on the mat with his weight on his forearms and knees and with his legs crossed. This resembles a seal-walk position. He then practices a right-leg high-leg over to one side, then a left-leg high-leg over to the other side *(figure A)*. To simulate an actual wrestling situation, the wrestler must at all times have his back arched to create proper hip pressure.

Coaching Points: This drill should then be done in partners. Determine the proper finish for the head and arm area.

8.22 Mount the Bull Contest

Skill Level: Peewee, junior high, senior high

Purpose: To develop skills needed to put legs on an opponent

Prerequisite: The wrestlers should be able to put legs on a partner in a drill situation.

Procedure: Wrestlers start in the up-down hover position, with one wrestler on his hands and knees and his partner standing behind him. The bottom man is the bull and the top man is the cowboy. The object of this game is for the cowboy to mount the bull by using an ankle pick and putting his front leg in for a grapevine ride *(figure A)*. This enhances the concept of using a far-ankle pick to put in legs. The bull attempts to run on his hands and knees to the opposite wall without being mounted.

Coaching Points: Do not allow the top men to use tackle maneuvers to mount. Insist that they use far-ankle picks with a leg going in to simulate an actual wrestling situation.

8.23 Helicopter Leg Drill

Skill Level: Junior high, senior high

Purpose: To use leg maneuvers to put an opponent into a near-fall position

Prerequisite: The wrestlers should have basic knowledge of various leg maneuvers used to score near-fall points.

Procedure: The defensive wrestler lies belly-down with this arms folded underneath his chest area. His hands lock on his own elbows. The top man starts with his legs in a cross-body ride position. The object is for the top wrestler to turn the bottom man past a 90-degree angle. The top man scores a point each time a tilt is scored. The roles are then reversed. The winner is the one who scores the most points in a given time period. In most cases, the top man uses a hip-over maneuver to get the bottom man over into the 90-degree position.

Coaching Points: Make sure that the bottom man locks his own elbows under his chest; he is not allowed to use his hands to defend.

Chapter **9**

BOTTOM MAN DRILLS

The drills in this chapter can be used to enhance a wrestler's ability to perform skills needed for executing successful escapes or reversals from the bottom referee's position in the traditional American folkstyle wrestling forum. The basic skills needed for success in the bottom position in folkstyle wrestling have not been as well defined as are the basic skills needed to successfully compete from the neutral position. It seems that the original seven basic skills identified by USA Wrestling have been designed to develop skills that enhance the wrestler's performance on their feet, the rationalization being that the better they perform on their feet, the better they will rank in international competitions.

In the 1992 edition there was preliminary discussion of the four basic skills needed from the down position. The definitions of these skills differed slightly from the definitions of those same skills as performed in the neutral position. Position, for instance, was defined as keeping arms tight to the sides, keeping forearms extended forward when broken down on the mat, and constantly reacting toward pressure from the top man (today some coaches teach going with pressure in an attempt to get to the feet). Motion will be created by continually executing move after move ("chaining moves"). Chaining should be considered a basic skill needed for success from the bottom. Examples of chain wrestling include the stand–switch and the sit-out and roll combinations. The basic skill of level change is used for such maneuvers as the stand-up, the Granby, and combinations of those maneuvers.

The final basic defensive skill discussed at the time was hand control: wrestlers were instructed to have control of one of the offensive wrestler's hands. This was thought to limit the attacks the offensive man might employ. However, throughout the early 2000's and into today's wrestling world, the "hand control" concept as a basic skill is being replaced by the defensive ability to simply "seal off."

This is a result of wrestlers' abilities becoming so proficient with tilts; a failed hand-control attempt may often result in a two-point or three-point near fall for the opponent. Coaches must make their own decisions regarding the use of hand control or a "seal off" as a basic skill of down wrestling. Hand control drills are still incorporated in the chapter.

The basic drills in this chapter include lead-up activities for sits, stand-ups, switches, and shoulder rolls and conclude with a series of chain wrestling activities such as floating (which incorporates chain wrestling by the bottom man and reaction wrestling by the offensive [top] man).

CHAPTER INDEX

9.1 Cat Drill

Skill Level: Peewee, junior high

Basic Skill: Position

Purpose: To condition a wrestler to fall to the mat in a belly-up position rather than falling to his back, in a potential pinning situation

Prerequisite: None

Procedure: If you imagine a cat being dropped from an upside-down position, you can immediately visualize the Cat Drill. The cat will always right itself and land in an upright position on its feet. The wrestler must learn to react in much the same manner. He must develop a sense of time and space and its relationship to the mat. For instance, a wrestler who is being taken down must learn to go "belly down" into a safe position rather than fall to his back, surrendering additional back points. *Figure A* shows the light wrestler holding his hands underneath dark's head in a position that prevents him from falling to the mat. The light wrestler then releases dark, allowing him to fall to the mat. Dark must react like a cat, righting himself into a referee's position on all fours, or at least into a belly-down position, before he hits the mat. This drill should help wrestlers learn that they must never fall to their backs.

Coaching Points: As the wrestlers become more proficient at this drill, you may want to increase the difficulty level by having the holder push down on the forehand of his partner.

9.2 Changeover Drill (Side change)

Skill Level: Peewee, junior high, senior high, college

Basic Skill: Position, motion

Purpose: To force the wrestler in the advantage position to change his position of attack.

Prerequisite: The wrestlers must be able to assume an up-down referee's position.

Procedure: This drill may be executed alone or with a partner. Here it will be described as executed with a partner to show dark's position change. The wrestlers begin in referee's position with dark on top and aligned on the "wrong side." The bottom (light) wrestler shifts his legs away from dark in a windshield-wiper-like motion and begins to sit back *(figure A)*. Light then lifts his hands from the mat and lets them pass in front of his face *(figure B)*. He continues this motion until his hands are place back on the mat, bringing himself into a referee's position *(figure C)*. The dark wrestler, in the advantage position, has now been forced to attack from the opposite side, thus allowing the light wrestler to work more comfortably for an escape or reversal.

Coaching Points: This maneuver is beneficial for any wrestler who feels uncomfortable wrestling an opponent who rides from the "wrong side." Encourage your wrestlers to execute a reversal or escape immediately following the changeover.

9.3 Changeover Drill (Pressure reaction) NEW

Skill Level: Peewee, junior high, senior high

Basic Skill: Chaining, position, motion

Purpose: To maintain a base and react to pressure while wrestling from the down position

Prerequisite: The wrestlers must be able to assume an up-down referee's position.

Procedure: The wrestler assumes an up-down referee's position. The top (advantage) wrestler attempts to break down the bottom wrestler by using a near arm chop and tight waist breakdown. **This then becomes a two count drill: 1.** The down wrestler (shown below) attempts to maintain his base, and **2.** He brings his right foot back to his buttocks *(figure A)* and then lifts and shifts his hips *(figure B)* creating the changeover. This will allow the defensive or light wrestler to then come to his feet.

Coaching Points: Again stress that a wrestler must react into pressure or he will have a hard time maintaining his base during competition.

9.4 Rock of Gibraltar Drill

Skill Level: Peewee, junior high, senior high

Basic Skill: Maintain base

Purpose: To maintain a base while wrestling from the down position

Prerequisite: The wrestlers must be able to assume an up-down referee's position.

Procedure: The wrestler assumes an up-down referee's position. The top (advantage) wrestler attempts to break down the bottom wrestler by forcing his hips to the mat. The top wrestler may use various types of attack–ankle picks, chops, spirals, and so on. The down wrestler attempts to maintain his base. He is allowed to counter only by using hand control, weight transfer, and changeovers.

Coaching Points: Stress that a wrestler must react into pressure or he will have a hard time maintaining his base during competition.

9.5 Tennis Ball-Hand Control Drill **REVISED**

Skill Level: Peewee, junior high

Basic Skill: Hand control

Purpose: To develop hand control for the bottom wrestler

Prerequisite: The bottom wrestler must be able to perform the basic maneuvers in this drill, such as sit-outs, stand-ups, rolls and switches.

Procedure: *Floating*: The top man puts a tennis ball in the hand he would put on his belly button when he is in referee's position. The bottom man then completes a series of moves (sit-outs, stand-ups, etc.) while attempting to hold on to the hand with the ball. This drill is meant to teach the bottom man the concept of hand control.

Sit and Granby Drills: This drill is similar to floating in the previous Tennis Ball Drill except that the bottom man attempts to control the hand with the ball while drilling the sit-back and Granby series. If a coach wants to attack the top hand, have the wrestler put the ball in that hand.

Coaching Points: This drill can be used two or three times a year to break up the monotony of regular practice sessions. It is especially effective for teaching the hand control concept to beginning or novice wrestlers.

9.6 Stand-Up Jack Drill

Skill Level: All levels

Basic Skill: Hand control or seal off

Purpose: To form a "seal off" position during a stand-up

Prerequisite: The wrestlers must be able to perform a stand-up.

Procedure: This is an individual drill in which wrestlers practice explosion from the bottom referee's position. The wrestler slaps his right shoulder with his left hand as he arches his back in an attempt to look at the wall behind him. His right hand meanwhile is reaching across his own belly button in an attempt to grab an opponent's wrist for hand control. The momentum of the back slap and arch should bring the wrestler's knees off the mat at least 6 to 12 inches *(figure A)*.

Coaching Points: You may wish to use this drill to develop explosive power before teaching the Frog-on-Fly Hand Control Drill (Drill 9.7).

9.7 Frog-on-Fly Hand Control Drill

Skill Level: Peewee, junior high

Basic Skill: Hand control

Purpose: To obtain hand control when performing a stand-up maneuver

Prerequisite: The wrestlers must be able to assume a bottom man referee's position.

Procedure: The wrestlers begin this drill in a normal up-down referee's position. The wresters are told that the top man's hand on the elbow is a fly. The down man's right hand is a frog. The light wrestler (down man) pushes off the mat using only his hands and a back-arching motion. He tries to slap his right shoulder with his left arm while pretending that his right hand forms a frog's mouth and will slide across to eat the fly *(figure A)*. Once the wrestlers grasp the concept of hand control, the drill can be expanded to include a stand-up.

Coaching Points: Once the frog has eaten the fly, instruct the kids to get two-on-one hand control. Then repeat the step until hand control becomes an automatic reaction.

9.8 Resistance Jack Drill

Skill Level: All levels

Basic Skill: Position, motion, hand control

Purpose: To add additional resistance to the back and neck areas for execution of the jack drills

Prerequisite: The wrestlers should participate in the Stand-Up Jack Drill (Drill 9.6) before adding resistance.

Procedure: The wrestlers begin this drill in a normal up-down referee's position. The wrestler with a sandbag on his neck area slaps his right shoulder with his left hand as he arches his back in an attempt to look at the wall behind him *(figure A)*. His right hand meanwhile is reaching across his own belly button in an attempt to grab an opponent's wrist for hand control. The momentum of the back slap and arch should bring the wrestler's knees off the mat at least 6 to 12 inches. In *(figure B)* the drill can be executed with a partner lying across the back of the wrestler standing up.

Coaching Points: This drill is designed for the wrestler to understand the concept of exploding with a back arch from the bottom position.

9.9 Hand-Fighting Hand Control Drill

Skill Level: All levels

Basic Skill: Position, motion, level change, hand control

Purpose: To obtain hand control from the stand-up position

Prerequisite: The wrestlers should have been exposed to previous drill.

Procedure: The light wrestler assumes a stand-up position with his left elbow in the V position tight to his hip and his right hand open but covering the dark wrestler's hand that is on his navel. The light wrestler's hips should also be arched away to create pressure on the opponent. The dark wrestler is in a rear standing position with his hands in the same position as if he were in top referee's position *(figure A)*.

The actual drill begins on a whistle command, with the dark wrestler attempting to lock his hands around the light wrestler's waist. The light wrestler attempts to block off and gain a two-on-one hand control. Normally the light wrestler attacks the hand that was on his elbow in the referee's position because he can easily catch it coming across his stomach.

Coaching Points: Once the bottom man develops hand control, you might wish to give the top man another option. Allow the top man to let the light wrestler fall to the mat or to chin him to the mat. This action will force the light wrestler to use the Cat Drill (Drill 9.1) to belly-down and prevent being "stuck" on his back.

9.10 Hand-Fighting Seal-Off Drill

Skill Level: All levels

Basic Skill: Position, motion, level change

Purpose: To form a "seal off" position during a stand-up

Prerequisite: The wrestlers must be able to perform a stand-up

Procedure: This drill differs from the preceding hand control drill only in that the bottom man attempts to seal off with his elbows and forearms, thus preventing the top man from locking around the waist. The coach may want the bottom man to finish the drill with a hip-heist cutoff maneuver.

Coaching Points: Wrestlers should be made to work from this laid back, arching position so that they learn to react to the movements of the top man. In fact, you may wish to have the rear standing wrestler on his hands and knees.

9.11 Wall Stand Drill

Skill Level: All levels

Basic Skill: Position, motion, hand control

Purpose: To practice the steps of a stand-up without a partner

Prerequisite: The wrestlers should have participated in the Jack Drills (Drills 9.6 & 9.8).

Procedure: The wrestler assumes a referee's position beside a wall. The wall acts as his opponent. This drill is the same as the stand-up jack drill, except the wrestler completes the stand-up. The wrestler steps up with his inside foot (the foot closet to the wall) and pivots away from the wall. The pivot action creates back pressure on the wall. The hips are well away from the wall *(figure A)*.

Coaching Points: You may want the wrestlers to stop in the wall-stand position to check for proper hip position and hand control. Or you might have the wrestlers do a hip heist to finish the stand-up.

9.12 Santa's Stuck in the Chimney Drill

Skill Level: Peewee, junior high

Basic Skill: Position, motion, level change

Purpose: To practice lowering the shoulders through an opponent's grasp

Prerequisite: None

Procedure: The light wrestler stands behind the dark wrestler with his arms circling dark's chest area. The dark wrestler has his hands up in the air, as if he were Santa Claus sliding down the chimney. The light wrestler tightens his grip, forcing Santa to get stuck. This forces the dark wrestler to dip his shoulder and squirm down through the light wrestler's grip, just as Santa would have to do if he were stuck in the chimney *(figure A)*.

Coaching Points: Tell the wrestlers that this is a simple "squirm drill."

9.13 All-Fours Hip Heist Drill

Skill Level: Peewee, junior high, senior high, college

Basic Skill: Position, motion chaining

Purpose: To practice the skill of a "low-leg under" or hip heist

Prerequisite: None

Procedure: A wrestler begins in a belly-up crab position with his weight supported on his hands and feet *(figure A)*. He crosses his left leg underneath his right leg *(figure B)*. This maneuver positions him into a belly-down-on-all-fours position, much the same as that of a defensive lineman *(figure C)*. The wrestler then crosses this right leg underneath his left leg, returning him to crab position *(figure D)*.

Coaching Points: Do not allow the wrestlers to sit on their buttocks during this drill.

9.14 Wall Sit–Hip Heist Drill

Skill Level: All levels

Basic Skill: Position, motion chaining

Purpose: To incorporate the hip heist as a finish for the stand-up maneuver

Prerequisite: The wrestlers must be able to perform a hip heist and a stand-up

Procedure: The wrestler sits on the floor with his back to the wall. On a whistle command, he arches back against the wall (in a motion similar to the force used in a stand-up) and executes a long sit-out to a hip heist *(figure A)*.

Coaching Points: This drill combines the ingredients of the sit back, stand-up, and hip heist into one drill. It should have effective carry over value for match situations.

9.15 Windshield Wiper Sits Drill

Skill Level: Peewee, junior high

Basic Skill: Position, motion

Purpose: To clear the legs to one side before performing a sit-back maneuver

Prerequisite: The wrestlers should be able to assume a down referee's position.

Procedure: The wrestlers assume down referee's positions without partners. On command, each wrestler sits his legs and feet to the side that would be away from an imaginary partner. This action resembles that of a windshield wiper and wipes them back and forth on the mat *(figure A)*. After they get the feel of the windshield wiper motion, have them use their hands to push back into a sit position.

Coaching Points: The key to this maneuver is encouraging the wrestlers to use their legs to move in a windshield wiper–type motion in order to clear them away from an opponent's attack.

9.16 Bridge-Around – High Leg Drill

Skill Level: Junior high, senior high, college

Basic Skill: Position, motion

Purpose: To be used as a lead-up for the tripod sit-out, and to enhance a wrestler's ability to execute a high-leg over maneuver from a bridging situation. This drill is used by the Soviets as a skill test for prospective elite wrestling candidates.

Prerequisite: The wrestlers must be able to perform a high-leg maneuver and a front and back bridge.

Procedure: This drill begins with a wrestler in a front bridge position. His hands are locked with a finger-chain grip in front of his face, and his elbows are flat on the mat. He begins to walk on his feet, rotating his body in a counterclockwise motion and maintaining the flat elbow position *(figure A)*. He rotates until he reaches a point at which the flat elbow position cannot be maintained unless a high-leg over is performed. The wrestler takes his left foot and steps over his right leg *(figure B)*. The high-leg maneuver positions him in a back bridge. The circular rotation continues until the flat elbow position once again cannot be maintained. At this point, the wrestler kicks his right foot over his left leg, returning to the front bridge position *(figure C)*. (This movement is similar to kicking a soccer ball in upside-down "Pelé style.") This concludes one full rotation for the bridge-around. The drill must be completed slowly at first; rotation speed is emphasized after technique and flexibility improve.

Coaching Points: Initially, wrestlers will want to raise their elbows off the mat. Insist that they maintain the flat elbow position during rotation, to obtain maximum flexibility.

9.17 Sit-Out and Roll-Even Drill

Skill Level: Peewee, junior high, senior high, college

Basic Skill: Position, motion, chaining

Purpose: To create a chaining action with a series of sit-outs

Prerequisite: Wrestlers must be able to perform a long sit-out.

Procedure: Each wrestler works without a partner, starting from a down referee's position. On a whistle command, the wrestler completes a long sit-out to one side, followed by another long sit-out to the opposite side. The routine continues for a given time period.

Coaching Points: Encourage your wrestlers to move as fast as possible and not to hesitate between moves. This drill can be used a part of a cardiovascular circuit workout such as PTA Drill (Drill 11.5). It is also a good exercise to use to practice floating.

9.18 Blindfold Drill

Skill Level: Peewee, junior high, senior high

Basic Skill: Position, motion, level change, chaining, hand control

Purpose: To develop a kinesthetic awareness of wrestling movements

Prerequisite: The wrestlers should be able to perform basic top and bottom man maneuvers.

Procedure: The down wrestler is blindfolded and instructed to execute various wrestling skills. This situation can include live wrestling as long as contact is maintained between wrestlers.

Coaching Points: The blindfold situation can also be used for wrestlers in the neutral position. However, the blind-start position should be used, and wrestlers must maintain contact throughout the drill.

Safety: Insist that once contact between wrestlers has broken, all combat must stop. Blind wrestling from a non-contact position could lead to potential injury.

9.19 Get Perpendicular Contest

Skill Level: All levels

Basic Skill: Position, motion

Purpose: To avoid being tilted by the top man

Prerequisite: The top man must be able to execute a tilt.

Procedure: The wrestlers start in an up-down referee's position. The top man attempts to tilt the bottom man, exposing his back to a 90-degree position, with a near arm-tight waist combination. The top man scores a point each time he accomplishes the 90-degree tilt. The bottom man attempts to get into a position perpendicular to the top man to avoid the tilt. The roles are reversed for the next time period.

Coaching Points: Insist that your wrestlers learn how to get themselves into a perpendicular position to avoid being tilted.

9.20 Shoulder Roll Drill

Skill Level: Peewee, junior high

Basic Skill: Position, motion

Purpose: To begin development of a shoulder roll

Prerequisite: None

Procedure:

1. **The wrestler sits on a crease of the mat.** He rolls to his left shoulder and pretends he is kicking a soccer ball with his right foot. This motion should bring him into a shoulder-shoulder position on the mat, and momentum brings him through to a sitting position. He should still be sitting on the crease of the mat, facing the same direction as when he started.

2. **The wrestler sits on the mat, placing his hands on his hips.** He rolls to the side, supporting himself with his neck, shoulders, and elbows.

Coaching Points: This is a good exercise to use to warm up the neck muscles before practice or live wrestling.

9.21 Flip Granby Drill

Skill Level: Peewee, junior high, senior high, college

Basic Skill: Position, motion, chaining

Purpose: To be used as a lead-up for a flip Granby maneuver

Prerequisite: Wrestlers should be able to perform a basic should roll.

Procedure: The emphasis for executing a flip Granby is to get the hips in an elevated position and kick a leg over one's head. This drill shows wrestlers how to accomplish that. The down wrester takes his left foot and steps it into a position in front of his right knee. He then steps his right foot behind the heel of the left foot. The hips are high off the mat *(figure A)*. The second phase is to kick the right leg straight up into a handstand – type position *(figure B)*. The wrestler completes the flip motion by tucking his head and throwing his left arm through and past his right knee.

Coaching Points: Insist that your wrestlers have their hips elevated. Have your wrestlers practice the first stage several times before performing the actual flip.

Safety Concerns: It is advisable to use a spotter when a wrestler is first attempting this skill. This would help insure that the wrestler not fall on his head and damage muscles in his neck.

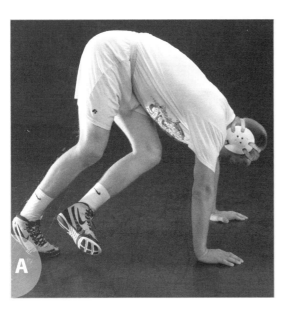

9.22 Ariel Flip Granby Drill

Skill Level: Junior high, senior high, college

Basic Skill: Position, motion, chaining

Purpose: The execute an aerial flip Granby from the stand-up position

Prerequisite: Wrestlers should be able to perform a simple cartwheel (one-handed) and a basic shoulder roll.

Procedure: The aerial flip Granby is simply a shoulder roll that is begun from the standing position. The wrestler takes two steps to the right, stops, changes direction by tucking his left shoulder, and flips in a shoulder-roll motion. The wrestler should practice the drill in three phases: using (if he wants to) his left hand to cartwheel when completing the flip *(figure A)*, then completing the drill by himself, and then completing the flip Granby with a partner.

Coaching Points: Be sure your wrestlers practice a simple shoulder roll and a regular Flip Granby before they try an Aerial Granby.

Safety Concerns: It is advisable to use a spotter when a wrestler is first attempting this skill. This would help insure that the wrestler not fall on his head and damage muscles in his neck.

9.23 Concede Takedown Drill

Skill Level: Junior high, senior high, college

Basic Skill: Position

Purpose: To make wrestlers realize that there are times when a takedown must be conceded in order to come to the mat in a "safe" position, preparing to score an immediate reversal

Prerequisite: The wrestlers must be able to perform a single leg takedown and wrist roll.

Procedure: The dark wrestler begins this drill by capturing a single leg on the light wrestler. The dark wrestler is instructed to score a takedown finish; the light wrestler is instructed to concede "at a point of no return." As the light wrestler concedes, he falls to a safe position on his knees with one hand near his side or belly button. This maneuver should bait dark to put his arm around light's waist and grab the hand that is on the belly button. This allows light to over control dark's hand with his opposite hand and executes a cross-arm wrist roll *(figure A)*. If the roll is not effective or if the top man does not control the hand around the waist, the light wrestler is at least in a safe position.

Coaching Points: Instruct you wrestlers to recognize when to give up a takedown and when to keep fighting off an attack. It is much more advantageous to give up a two-point takedown with the possibility of an immediate reversal than it is to give up five points and be fighting off one's back.

9.24 Switch–Elevator Drill

Skill Level: Junior high, senior high

Basic Skill: Position, motion, chaining

Purpose: To effectively score against an opponent who steps over a leg in an attempt to stop a switch maneuver

Prerequisite: The wrestlers must be able to perform a basic switch and an elevator maneuver

Procedure: The light wrestler executes a switch, and dark counters by stepping over and between light's legs. The dark wrestler has his head down and hips up in the air. Light kicks up through dark's crotch, lifting dark's hips and forcing him into a somersault *(figure A)*. When first attempting this maneuver, the wrestler should elevate his opponent several times without kicking him over into a somersault. Once this skill has been learned, light elevates and uses his right calf to catch behind dark's knee *(figure B)*. The movements of dark's somersault pull light over on top. Light then scrambles for a near fall with any catch-as-catch-can maneuver.

Coaching Points: The end of this drill can be particularly useful in teaching wrestlers how to scramble in a catch-as-catch-can situation. Caution wrestlers against lying on or nearly on their backs for an extended period while attempting to elevate, because some referee's will count back points.

9.25 Switch and Reswitch Chain Drills

Skill Level: All levels

Basic Skill: Position, motion, chaining, hand control

Purpose: To practice the switch, and switch counter, in a chaining situation

Prerequisite: The wrestlers must be able to perform all components of the chain: outside-leg reswitch, inside-leg reswitch, hip heist and bear crawl

Procedure:

Switch–Outside-Leg Reswitch: The light wrestler executes a switch. The dark wrestler counters by lifting his leg and sitting away from the light wrestler *(figure A)*. The wrestlers continue to switch–reswitch routine.

Switch–Reswitch–Roll Chain: The light wrestler executes a switch, and dark counters by sitting to the outside for a reswitch. Dark thinks he has successfully countered light's switch attempt. As dark begins to come up top to maintain control, light uses his right elbow to lock onto dark's elbow, does a right-shoulder dive *(figure B)* and then hips over for the score *(figure C)*.

Switch–Inside-Leg Reswitch: This drill is the same as the switch–outside-leg re-switch except the re-switch man (the dark wrestler) sits underneath and into his opponent *(figure D)*. Many wrestlers use this method even though it can be easily countered by a hip heist-bear crawl. The wrestlers continue a switch – reswitch routine.

Switch–Inside Reswitch-Hip Heist-Bear Crawl: This drill carries the last drill one step further. The inside-leg reswitch is countered by the light wrestler executing a right-leg hip heist *(figure E)* and then using a bear crawl toward the head, securing a half nelson and crotch body press *(figure F)*

Coaching Points: This switch series of reaction drills can also be incorporated into a floating exercise.

9.26 Sit-Back Reaction Drill REVISED

Skill Level: Junior high, senior high, college

Basic Skill: Position, motion, chaining, hand control

Purpose: To teach a wrestler the proper method of scoring from the sit-back position depending upon the top man's actions

Prerequisite: The wrestlers should be able to perform the reactions involved in this drill

Procedure: The bottom man does a sit-back into his partner while maintaining control of the hand on his belly button. The coach then designates the movement the top man should use to stop the sit-back. The bottom man then uses that movement to score. **A series of action–reaction situations might include the following:**

Top Man Action	Bottom Man Reaction for Score
1. Hang arm over shoulder	Fan out to side
2. Hang head over shoulder	Fan and catch head
3. Near-arm chop	Shoulder roll or tripod
4. Near-arm chop follow-around	Tripod to Peterson roll
5. Force pressure into back	Stand-up
6. Chin back	Scoot back to maintain base
7. Arm bar	Hand control and arm drag

Coaching Points: You may want to design a different system for reaction to the top man and drill it so that it will become automatic when the situations occur.

Chapter **10**

GAMES & MAT ACTIVITIES

This chapter contains many games and other activities that can be played on a wrestling mat and will give peewee and junior high school wrestlers a great deal of emotional and physical pleasure. Even the most advanced high school wrestler will find most of these activities to be a welcome relief from the normal rigors of daily training. The physical educator would be able to use many of these games and activities for a basic combative class.

The activities fall into three major categories:

A *Individual or dual wrestling-related* contests, such as 10.12 Sumo Wrestling, featuring one-on-one competitions using the basic skills of wrestling.

B *Team wrestling contests,* such as 10.29 Rodeo, involving team-concept competition using basic wrestling skills.

C *Activities that have been modified* to be played on a wrestling mat, such as 10.38 Knee Football. Although these types of activities don't teach new wrestling skills, they do give wrestlers relaxing and enjoyable diversions from the monotony of daily practice.

Peewee and junior high school programs should provide a "have fun" atmosphere, and wrestling-related games are one way to accomplish that goal. The activities in this chapter can be used to promote the sport of wrestling and hopefully to recruit future participants. Wrestlers at the higher levels will find them a welcome addition to the normal regime of daily training. All of these activities can be revised to meet the needs of your program.

CHAPTER INDEX

10.1 Chain Tag NEW

Skill Level: Peewee, junior high

Basic Skill: N/A

Purpose: Movement and to have fun on a mat

Prerequisite: None

Procedure: All wrestlers are assigned to stay inside a designated area such as inside the big circle on a mat. One wrestler is assigned to tag the other wrestlers. Once a wrestler is tagged he must lock elbows with the tagger. They will continue to tag people and lock elbows until all but one wrestler is tagged.

Coaching Points: None

10.2 Turtle Back NEW

Skill Level: Peewee, junior high

Basic Skill: Position

Purpose: To engage in a top/bottom contest within a confined area. The object of this contest is to practice tilting an opponent.

Prerequisite: The wrestlers should have a basic competence in performing top-bottom position scoring maneuvers.

Procedure: All wrestlers face off in the big circle. Wrestlers must remain on their knees as they face off. The objective is to obtain an advantage position and score a tilt or turn an opponent to their back. Once a wrestler has been tilted they go to the outside of the circle and practice takedowns.

Coaching Points: Attempt to group combatants by weight classifications, (i.e., light-weights, middleweights, and heavyweights).

10.3 Body Crawl

Skill Level: Junior high, senior high, college

Basic Skill: N/A

Purpose: To cling and climb on and around another person's body

Prerequisite: None

Procedure: The light wrestler stands on the mat with his arms bent at the elbows and his forearms extending forward. The dark wrestler jumps on the waist of the light wrestler. The objective is for the dark wrestler to crawl up and over the light wrestler's head and shoulders, down his back, through his crotch, and back to the starting position *(figure A)*. He must do this without touching the mat with any part of his body.

Coaching Points: The toughest phase of this exercise is getting the legs through the crotch area without touching the mat. In most cases the foundation man should be slightly larger than his partner due to the strength needed for maintaining a solid base. This skill can be used as a game to see who can actually execute the skill, or it can be a contest of speed.

10.4 Chin and Head Duck Contest

Skill Level: Junior high, senior high, college

Basic Skill: Position, penetration, lifting

Purpose: To use head rotation and a "looking up" motion when using a duckunder

Prerequisite: The wrestlers should be able to perform a duckunder maneuver from the neutral position.

Procedure: The wrestlers both use their right hands to go over each other's neck and hold onto their partner's chin *(figure A)*. They are both on their knees. The contest is to see who can put the other to his back first, using this grip and head position. Each wrestler may let one knee come off the mat and use a foot for support.

Coaching Points: Caution your wrestlers not to use a neck wrench when grabbing the chin. They may use only head and neck rotation to score.

10.5 Squat Back Wrestling

Skill Level: Peewee, junior high, senior high

Basic Skill: Position, motion, level change, penetration, backstep, lifting, back arch

Purpose: To engage in a "scramble wrestling" situation

Prerequisite: The wrestlers should be able to perform basic wrestling maneuvers.

Procedure: The wrestlers assume a back-to-back squat position *(figure A)*. They must be leaning against each other to stay on their feet. On the whistle, live wrestling occurs.

Coaching Points: This is another game that is useful both in physical education class and as a scramble wrestling situation in the practice room. Encourage the wrestlers to score immediately after facing one another.

Safety Concerns: Make sure the contest are properly divided into lightweight, middleweight and heavyweight classes.

10.6 Chicken Fighting

Skill Level: Peewee, junior high

Basic Skill: Position, motion

Purpose: To develop balance in a competitive setting

Prerequisite: None

Procedure: The wrestlers are directed to score takedowns while hopping on one foot *(figure A)*. Each wrestler must hold one leg up with a hand and use the free hand for combat; using drags, shucks and shrugs, he tries to knock his opponent from his feet.

Coaching Points: You may wish to allow each wrestler to hop but not hold up his foot. This would allow the wrestlers to use both hands and the free leg to block and trip with. The wrestler would then be able to use foot sweeps and trips for takedowns.

Safety Concerns: Make sure the contest are properly divided into lightweight, middleweight and heavyweight classes.

10.7 Log Roll Game (Down)

Skill Level: Peewee, junior high

Basic Skill: Position, motion, level change, backstep, lifting, back arch

Purpose: To engage in a scramble wrestling situation

Prerequisite: The wrestlers should possess competence in performing basic scoring maneuvers.

Procedure: Wrestlers lie side by side with a 5-foot space between them. Each wrestler has his head even with the other's feet. The wrestlers are instructed to roll toward each other and to commence live wrestling as soon as they make contact.

Coaching Points: Emphasize that the wrestlers are not to commence live wrestling until contact has been made. This game provides an excellent situation for practicing scramble wrestling. It may also be used as an activity for physical education class.

10.8 Log Roll Live (Feet)**NEW**

Skill Level: Junior high, high school, college

Basic Skill: Position, motion, level change

Purpose: To engage in a scramble wrestling situation

Prerequisite: The wrestlers should possess competence in performing basic scoring maneuvers.

Procedure: All wrestlers face each other on one side of the mat and begin to move in a proper stance toward the center. On command both wrestlers are instructed to go to the mat completing a log roll *(figure A)*. Wrestlers are to commence live wrestling once the log roll is completed.

Coaching Points: Emphasize that the wrestlers are not to commence live wrestling until the roll has been completed. This game provides an excellent situation for practicing scramble wrestling. It may also be used as an activity for physical education class.

10.9 Somersault Scramble (Feet) NEW

Skill Level: Junior high, high school, college

Basic Skill: Position, motion, level change

Purpose: To engage in a scramble wrestling situation

Prerequisite: The wrestlers should possess competence in performing basic scoring maneuvers.

Procedure: Wrestlers face each other approximately 10-15 feet apart from each other. On command the wrestlers are instructed to complete a forward roll, rolling toward each other. Wrestlers are to commence live wrestling once the forward roll is completed.

Coaching Points: Emphasize that the wrestlers are not to commence live wrestling until the roll has been completed. This game provides an excellent situation for practicing scramble wrestling. It may also be used as an activity for physical education class.

CAUTION: Be sure that wrestlers are far enough apart so that they don't roll into each other during the forward roll.

10.10 Knee Sumo Wrestling I (Push out) NEW

Skill Level: Peewee, junior high

Basic Skill: Position

Purpose: To engage in a takedown contest within a confined area. This contest contains a sumo wrestling element because the contest can be won by throwing the opponent from the circle.

Prerequisite: The wrestlers should have a basic competence in performing neutral-position scoring maneuvers.

Procedure: Two wrestlers face off in a 10-foot (or smaller) circle. Wrestlers must remain on their knees and keep their hands locked behind their back. The objective is to push each other out of the circle. The first wrestler to touch outside the circle is the loser.

Coaching Points: This can be used to match individual wrestling skills, and it is no more dangerous than any other combative exercise.

10.11 Knee Sumo Wrestling II (Tip over) NEW

Skill Level: Peewee, junior high,

Basic Skill: Position

Purpose: To engage in a takedown contest within a confined areas for instance the big circle. This contest contains a sumo wrestling element because the contest can be won by throwing the opponent from the circle or by taking an opponent to their back from their knees.

Prerequisite: The wrestlers should have a basic competence in obtaining and performing an upper body overhook/underhook position.

Procedure: Have wrestlers face off in the big circle on the mat. Wrestlers must remain on their knees and will face off with one opponent at a time. The objective is to push the wrestler out of the circle or tip the opponent to their back. The wrestler who touches the line of the circle or is tipped to his back will go to the outside of the circle and begin pummeling with a partner until the game concludes.

Coaching Points: This can be used to match individual wrestling skills, and it is no more dangerous than any other combative exercise.

10.12 Sumo Wrestling

Skill Level: Peewee, junior high, senior high, college

Basic Skill: Position, motion, level change, penetration, back step, lifting, back arch

Purpose: To engage in a takedown contest within a confined area. This contest contains a sumo wrestling element because the contest can be won by throwing the opponent from the circle.

Prerequisite: The wrestlers should have a basic competence in performing neutral-position scoring maneuvers.

Procedure: Two wrestlers face off in a 10-foot circle. The objective is to push each other out of the circle or to score a takedown inside the circle. The first wrestler to touch outside the circle is the loser unless a takedown has been scored. Many times a wrestler who is being pushed out will use a lateral drop or headlock to score and end up the winner.

Coaching Points: This can be used to match individual wrestling skills, and it is no more dangerous than any other combative exercise.

10.13 Knee Combat Contest

Skill Level: Peewee, junior high, senior high

Basic Skill: Position, motion, level change, penetration

Purpose: This contest is designated to practice skills used when wrestling a man who is on both knees in the neutral position

Prerequisite: The wrestlers should possess the competence to perform basic scoring maneuvers from the neutral position

Procedure: One wrestler must stay on both knees and defend himself from being taken down. He may not step up with a foot for balance. The other wrestler uses any takedown available to score. The roles are then reversed. Whoever scores the most takedowns in a certain time period is the winner.

Coaching Points: Wrestlers will have the most success by using a series of snaps, shucks and shrug maneuvers to score.

10.14 Mat Wars (Teams) **NEW**

Skill Level: Peewee, junior high, senior high

Purpose: To practice wrestling from the neutral position while upright on one's knees

Prerequisite: The wrestlers should be able to perform basic wrestling maneuvers

Procedure: Similar to the above game except the contest is competed by teams of five. The team that scores a minimum of three victories will remain in the contest. Have 5 v 5 contests until champion is crowned. Teams losing can practice takedowns until the contest is complete.

Coaching Points: Be cautious about letting lightweight wrestlers compete with heavyweight wrestlers. It is suggested that champions be crowned in each of the three divisions. Advise your wrestlers that all competition must be in one-on-one situations.

10.15 Dead Cockroach

Skill Level: Peewee, junior high

Basic Skill: Position, motion, level change, penetration, back step, lifting, back arch

Purpose: To have fun and to engage in a scramble wrestling situation

Prerequisite: The wrestlers should possess competence in performing basic scoring maneuvers from the up-down referee's position

Procedure: The game begins with wrestlers lying side by side in the head-to-feet position. They are instructed to imagine themselves as cockroaches. The coach tells them that he is going to spray them with insecticide. As he pretends to do this, they are to act like dying cockroaches—complete with convulsions and trembling limbs. Then on a whistle command, they wrestle live. Kids have great fun playing this game.

Coaching Points: This is a great game, but you must give it great buildup before starting. It can be used in the peewee practice room or in elementary and junior high physical education classes.

10.16 Horses in the Barn **NEW**

Skill Level: Peewee, junior high

Purpose: To have fun and to engage in a scramble wrestling situation

Prerequisite: The wrestlers should possess competence in performing basic scoring maneuvers from the up-down referee's position

Procedure: The game begins with wrestlers side by side on their hands and knees as in a down referee's position. They are instructed to imagine themselves as horses standing in a stall in a barn. The coach tells them that on the whistle they must buck and kick with both feet. Once they complete the kick, they wrestle live. Kids have great fun playing this game.

Coaching Points: This is a great game, but you must give it great buildup before starting. It can be used in the peewee practice room or in elementary and junior high physical education classes.

10.17 The Cross Drill (Chest) **NEW**

Skill Level: Peewee, junior high, senior high

Purpose: To have fun and to engage in a scramble wrestling situation

Prerequisite: The wrestlers should possess competence in performing basic half nelson skills and basic knowledge for getting off one's back from the up-down referee's position.

Procedure: The contest begins with wrestlers lying in a plus sign (+) position. The top wrestler lays across the bottom mans chest and must have his elbows in the far side of the bottom man. The bottom man must have his arms extended. Then on a whistle command, they wrestle live. Kids have great fun playing this game.

Coaching Points: This is a great contest for wrestlers to work on pinning and for getting off of their backs. It can be used in the peewee practice room or in elementary and junior high physical education classes.

10.18 The Cross Drill (Legs) **NEW**

Skill Level: Peewee, junior high, senior high

Purpose: To have fun and to engage in a scramble wrestling situation

Prerequisite: The wrestlers should possess competence in performing basic skills from the up-down referee's position.

Procedure: The contest begins with wrestlers lying in a plus sign (+) position. The top wrestler lays across the bottom mans legs and must have his elbows in the far side of the bottom man. The bottom man must have his arms extended. Then on a whistle command, they wrestle live. Kids have great fun playing this game.

Coaching Points: This is a great contest for wrestlers to work on pinning and for getting off of their backs. It can be used in the peewee practice room or in elementary and junior high physical education classes.

10.19 Zone Drill

Skill Level: Junior high, senior high

Basic Skill: Position, motion, level change, penetration, back step, lifting, back arch

Purpose: To keep wrestlers inbounds and out of the zone area in Freestyle and Greco-Roman wrestling

Prerequisite: The wrestlers should be able to maintain a proper stance and create motion.

Procedure:

Freestyle – Greco-Roman Drill: One wrestler is placed with his feet on or near, and his back toward, the out-of-bounds line. On command, they wrestler on the inside attempts to force the other to stay close to the line or go out of bounds. The wrestler with his back to the circle must turn his opponent so that his opponent's back is to the outside. He may use snaps, shucks or shrugs to turn his opponent.

Folkstyle Drill: In folkstyle wrestling, the offensive wrestler wants his back to the out-of bounds line so that he may penetrate across the entire mat (if needed) for a score. However, wrestlers are not allowed to "play the edge of the mat."

Coaching Points: This is an excellent drill for preparing wrestlers for Freestyle or Greco-Roman competition.

10.20 Steal the Dragon's Tail

Skill Level: Peewee, junior high

Basic Skill: Position, motion, level change, penetration

Purpose: To utilize various wrestling techniques needed for a match situation, but in a game-like atmosphere

Prerequisite: The wrestlers should be able to perform basic scoring maneuvers in the neutral position.

Procedure: The game begins with each wrestler tucking a sock into the back of his wrestling shorts. The sock should hang out at least 6 – 8 inches. The coach then gives a command, such as "the game is to steal the dragon's tail by using a high-crotch maneuver." The wrestler who steals the opponent's sock by executing a high crotch would be the winner. There are other maneuvers that could be used in Steal the Dragon's Tail: arm drags, snap downs, duck-under to prevent a free-for-all instance.

Coaching Points: Insist that the wrestlers let the socks hang out of their shorts at least 6 inches. Some wrestlers may attempt to tie the sock to their jock to avoid losing the competition. This is unacceptable for the obvious reason.

10.21 Simon Says – Wall Squat Game

Skill Level: Peewee, junior high

Purpose: To develop cognitive (thinking and reaction) faculties under physical stress

Prerequisite: None

Procedure: One wrestler assumes a squat position against a wall on a wrestling mat. His opponent faces him and becomes "Simon" for a 3-minute Simon Says game. For example, the Simon wrestler will say, "Simon says, 'Touch your left knee with your right hand,'" simultaneously touching his own left knee with right hand. The wrestler on the wall will then perform the proper movement. If the wrestler on the wall makes a movement not described by Simon, his opponent scores one point. The roles are then reversed for another 3-minute time period. The movements Simon picks might include backslaps, hand control, snap motions, drag motion, or tapping of various body parts.

Coaching Points: This game will help to build endurance in the quadriceps muscles of a wrestler and hopefully help him to maintain a proper stance throughout an entire match. The wrestler who scores the most points by fooling his partner should receive some type of reward after practice. This game can be used to conclude a wrestling practice or for physical education class. While this game is being played you may wish to elaborate on the importance of maintaining a proper stance late in a match.

10.22 Balmert's Matoploy

Skill Level: Junior high, senior high

Basic Skill: Position, motion, level change, penetration, back step, lifting, back arch

Purpose: To provide a break from the daily practice routine, while including many of the wrestling skills and physical exercises of a regular practice

Prerequisite: The wrestlers should have a basic competence in all wrestling technique maneuvers.

Procedure: This game is played using a normal Monopoly board. A coach must take pieces of tape and re-label, as follows, the board properties, utilities, and railroads, and so on–these will be bought by the wrestlers with exercises instead of money.

Board Space	Cost
Vermont Avenue	20 sit-ups
Connecticut Avenue	25 sit-ups
Oriental Avenue	20 sit-ups
St. Charles Place	25 push-ups
States Avenue	25 push-ups
Virginia Avenue	30 push-ups
Pacific Avenue	25 squat thrusts
North Carolina Avenue	25 squat thrusts
Pennsylvania Avenue	30 squat thrusts
Indiana Avenue	10 pull-ups
Illinois Avenue	12 pull-ups
Kentucky Avenue	10 pull-ups
Marvin Gardens	25 grass drills
Atlantic Avenue	25 grass drills
Ventnor Avenue	30 grass drills
St. James Place	25 squat jumps
Tennessee Avenue	25 squat jumps
New York Avenue	30 squat jumps
Boardwalk	25 6-count squat thrusts
Park Place	25 6-count squat thrusts
Mediterranean Avenue	25 mountain climbers
Baltic Avenue	25 mountain climbers
Railroads	3 bear crawls, length of the room
Luxury Tax & Income Tax	20 reverse push-ups
Any utility	Leap frogs - twice the amount on dice throw
Go	Get free drink
Just visiting jail	10 jumping jacks
In jail	Fight off back

The Chance and Community Chest cards should be labeled with various skills, such as the following:

- Hit 5 doubles
- 5 cradle finishes
- Do 5 firearms
- Do 5 duck-unders
- 5 arm drags
- 5 ankle picks
- 5 singles to right side
- Get off back-5 bridge and turns
- 5 hip drags
- 5 single finishes off mat

- 5 sit backs
- 5 high crotches
- 5 stand ups
- 5 finishes off two-on-one
- 5 head snaps
- 5 headlocks
- 5 team assigned drills
- 5 high halfs
- 5 single finishes on mat (head inside)

The rules are very simple. The wrestlers are divided into two teams, and "coaches" or "captains" roll the dice. Each time a team lands on a property or utility they must pay for it by doing the prescribed exercises; if that team lands on that property again, they can put a house on it for another set of exercises. If a team lands on a property owned by the opponents, they have to do double the prescribed exercises if there are not house on it, 3 times the exercises for one house and 4 times the exercises for two houses. A team must land on Go to get a drink. The game should be played 2 hours, with the losing team rolling up the mats or with the winning team getting refreshment such as fruit or a fruit drink.

Coaching Points: This would be a great game to play using the varsity against the junior varsity. Don't use this game more than once or twice a season, as it might become boring.

This game was developed by Coach Mickey Balmert
of Bishop Ready High School, Columbus, Ohio

10.23 Cradle-Grip Circle Game

Skill Level: Peewee, junior high, senior high

Basic Skill: N/A

Purpose: To improve the grip a wrestler would use to apply a cradle

Prerequisite: Wrestlers should be able to lock their hands using either a wrestler's grip (cupped hands) or finger-chain grip.

Procedure: Twelve wrestlers sit in a circle with their feet pointing to the inside of the circle. They interlock their arms with the arms of the wrestlers next to them and lock their own hands; this forms a complete chain around the circle. Wrestlers are told to pretend that they have a cradle locked up and that they should attempt to bring their elbows close together to tighten the grip. At this point, the wrestlers lean back and lie on their backs. Any wrestler whose grip is broken is eliminated from the circle and assigned to pummel or spar until the contest concludes. This activity continues until there are only two wrestlers left in the circle. Another way for a wrestler to be eliminated is by being pulled off the mat and onto his feet. This might occur once there are only three wrestlers left in the circle.

Coaching Points: This game is relatively safe at all levels. Most players will break their grip before any injury would occur to shoulder or arms.

10.24 Mat Tug-of-War

Skill Level: Peewee, junior high

Basic Skill: N/A

Purpose: To simply have fun on a wrestling mat

Prerequisite: None

Procedure: The wrestlers are divided into two teams, separated by a line (usually the line will be where sections of the mat are taped together). All wrestlers must stay on their hands and knees. The object of this game is for members of one team to pull the members of the other team across the line. Once a wrestler has been pulled completely across the line, he must sit against the wall. The wall is "jail" until the game is complete. The rules are very simple: no biting, scratching, or standing up to pull a wrestler across the line. Teammates are not allowed to help each other defend against being pulled across the line.

Coaching Points: Make sure that the wrestlers do not stand up on their feet to pull an opponent.

10.25 Towel Tug-of-War **NEW**

Skill Level: Peewee, junior high

Basic Skill: N/A

Purpose: To simply have fun on a wrestling mat

Prerequisite: None

Procedure: Start with a rolled towel, then wrap three pieces of tape around the towel to keep it rolled up. Place the towel in the center of the mat. Split the group into two groups and then number off each person on each side. When coach calls your number run out and get the towel back to your side using speed, strength, and technique.

Coaching Points: Wrestlers may stand up on their feet to pull an opponent.

10.26 Cowboys and Indians

Skill Level: Peewee, junior high

Purpose: To practice maintaining a base for the bottom man and riding for the top man

Prerequisite: None

Procedure: The top men mount up as if they were riders on horses. They must be in a crab-leg fashion with toes tucked in the horse's (down man's) calves. The contest is to knock other riders off of their horses or to knock the horses off of their bases. The top man (rider) is not allowed to put his feet on the mat to maintain a base. Once the wrestlers are knocked down, they must go to the side of the mat until a winner has been determined. This contest can be individual or in teams such as cowboys and Indians.

Coaching Points: Do not allow wrestlers to put their feet on the mat. Discourage ganging up (several riders against one rider).

10.27 Sharks and Minnows

Skill Level: Peewee, junior high

Purpose: To develop upper body movement skills

Prerequisite: The wrestlers should possess basic knowledge of the wrestling skills needed for this contest.

Procedure: The game begins with four wrestlers in the middle of the wrestling room upright on their knees; they are the "sharks." The rest of the wrestlers line up next to a wall, also on their knees; they are the "minnows." The object of the game is for the minnows to cross the room on their knees without sharks attacking them and exposing their backs to the mat. If the shark attacks a minnow and exposes his back to the mat, that minnow then becomes a shark. The minnows continue crossing the mat until there is only one left. He is the winner.

This game can also be played in teams. A team or "school" of sharks would consist of six wrestlers. In this case, the minnows simply see how many times in a two-minute period they can cross the mat without having their backs exposed to the mat. In this team version, the exposed wrestlers sit off to the side after they have been exposed. After two minutes the next school of sharks goes into the middle. The winning team is decided by how many minnow's backs were exposed in each two-minute time period.

Coaching Points: You may also changes techniques to be used by the sharks; for example, sharks might score only using headlocks, or they might tilt rather than expose backs, to score. This can be a team wrestling game or a physical education activity game.

10.28 King, Queens, Jacks **NEW**

Skill Level: Peewee, junior high

Purpose: To develop upper body movement skills

Prerequisite: The wrestlers should possess basic knowledge of the wrestling skills needed for this contest.

Procedure: Split your team into three groups. Name each team Kings, Queens, or Jacks. Coach picks one wrestler to go to the middle of the mat. When the person in the middle calls a group's name, that group has to run to the other side. The object of the person in the middle is to grab a hold of a runner and lift their feet off the ground and set them back down, much like picking up a jack in the game of jacks. Once that occurs, that person joins the man in the middle. (To complete on knees, man in middle has to gain control.)

Coaching Points: This can be a team wrestling game or a physical education activity game. Remind participants that they are to lift people off of the mat and not to tackle them.

10.29 Rodeo

Skill Level: Junior high, senior high, college

Basic Skill: Position, motion

Purpose: To practice tilting an opponent while having fun in a game-like situation

Prerequisite: The wrestlers must be able to perform basic tilts from referee's position

Procedure: Six wrestlers are needed. There are two teams, each consisting of a horse, rider and bull. Two wrestlers are down on all fours (they are horses), two are riders (they are the cowboys), and another two are down on all fours (they are the bulls). The object of the game is for each team's rider and horse to approach the other team's bull and attempt to bulldog him to the mat. The first rider to jump from his horse onto a bull and successfully bulldog him into a tilt position is the winner.

Coaching Points: This is a good game to play at camp or during a light day at practice. The kids will love it.

10.30 Mat Chess

Skill Level: Peewee, junior high

Basic Skill: N/A

Purpose: To have fun on a wrestling mat during a crash course in chess

Prerequisite: None

Procedure: The game consists of two teams of 16 people each. The teams face each other in the following formation:

Front Line: Eight wrestlers on their hands and knees. These are the pawns and can go anywhere on the mat as long as they stay on all fours.

Second Line: Seven wrestlers up-right on their knees. These wrestlers are the bishops, knights, rooks and queen; they also can go anywhere on the mat as long as they stay on their knees.

Third Line: One wrestler standing on his feet. He is the king and can go anywhere on the mat.

The object of the game is to capture the opponent's king and bring him to the mat.

Coaching Points: Play the game seven or eight times and encourage the teams to develop strategies for protecting their own king while attempting to capture their opponent's king.

Safety Concerns: There is a slight risk of kids' falling on each other; however, most will slip away from any danger zone. Do not allow the king to use a wall to hold himself upright – if he does that, stop play immediately and declare the opposing team winner of that game.

10.31 Crab Kills

Skill Level: Peewee, junior high

Basic Skill: N/A

Purpose: To enhance endurance of the arm muscles while having fun on the wrestling mat

Prerequisite: None

Procedure: All of the wrestlers in the room are to assume belly-up crab positions with their weight supported on their hands and feet. The object of the game is to force an opposing wrestler to touch his buttocks on the mat, eliminating him. The last wrestler remaining in the crab position is the winner. The wrestlers may trip another wrestler, pull his arms out from under him, or just ram an opponent to force him down on his buttocks.

Coaching Points: The participants must not be allowed to kick during this game. This is an excellent activity for wrestling practice or physical education classes.

10.32 Medicine Ball Games

Skill Level: Junior high, senior high

Basic Skill: N/A

Purpose: To have fun on a wrestling mat and possibly develop some muscular endurance

Prerequisite: None

Procedure:

Wrestle for the Ball: In this game a medicine ball is placed in a circle with two wrestlers. The contest is to see who can control the ball and carry it out of the circle.

Rugby Ball: There are two teams in a room with a medicine ball. The object is to get the ball to one end or the other of the room. The wrestlers must stay on their knees and may only carry, throw or roll the ball (and may not bite, pinch, scratch, etc.).

Neck Isometrics: This is a simple conditioning drill in which a wrestlers puts the ball on the mat and lays his head on it in a belly-up position. He then straightens his body so that only his feet are on the mat. This is an excellent neck exercise. It is best used in a circuit training drill.

Coaching Points: The rugby ball might be better suited for a physical education class, but wrestling for the ball and using the ball for neck isometrics are excellent wrestling-related activities.

10.33 Stick Wrestling Contests

Skill Level: Peewee, junior high, senior high, college

Basic Skill: N/A

Purpose: To develop muscular strength throughout a desired range of motion during combative exercise

Prerequisite: None

Procedure:

Right Tip Down: Two wrestlers stand facing each other and holding a stick over their heads. On command, each wrestler attempts to push then end of the stick that's at his left side in an upward motion and the end that's to his right in a downward motion *(figure A)*. This same contest could be executed with the stick held at waist or chest level.

Lift the Partner: Two wrestlers grasp a heavy stick at thigh level. On command, one wrestler attempts to lift the stick over his head while the other opposes. Roles are reversed for the next time session.

Pullover: Two wrestlers stand back to back holding a stick overhead. On command, each wrestler attempts to bring the stick down in front of his chest *(figure B)*. This action will pull his opponent over his back.

Coaching Points: Use a stick that is heavy enough not to break during competition. A shovel handle might serve well for this exercise. These types of activities might be included as a station in circuit training.

10.34 Force the Elbows

Skill Level: Junior high, senior high, college

Basic Skill: N/A

Purpose: To be used as isometric exercises to develop strength in the shoulder and arm areas

Prerequisite: The wrestlers should participate in numerous flexibility exercises before engaging in this contest.

Procedure: A wrestler locks his hands behind his head and leans against a wall in a squat position. His elbows are pointing toward his partner, who is standing directly in front of him (*figure A*). The contest is to see how long it takes the partner to push the squatting wrestler's elbow against the mat on the wall.

Coaching Points: Instruct your wrestlers to push the elbows in a slow, steady manner in their first contests.

10.35 Handshake Wrestling

Skill Level: Peewee, junior high, senior high

Basic Skill: N/A

Purpose: To exhibit power and balance in a combative setting

Prerequisite: None

Procedure: Wrestlers face each other, use a "shaking hands" grip, and place their right feet side by side. The object is to force the opponent to move either of his feet or to touch the mat with a hand or knee.

Coaching Points: This exercise is useful at the end of practice or as a physical education activity. Other grips, such as hand-on-elbow, could be used for this contest.

10.36 Leg Wrestle

Skill Level: Peewee, junior high, senior high

Basic Skill: N/A

Purpose: To have fun on a wrestling mat

Prerequisite: None

Procedure: The wrestler lie side by side with their heads pointing in opposite directions and their right elbows hooked. They raise their right legs three times, each time bumping their knees together. The third time, they hook their legs at the knee and attempt to force each other into a backward roll.

Coaching Points: Make sure that competing wrestlers are similar in weight.

10.37 Circle Games

Skill Level: Peewee, junior high, senior high

Basic Skill: N/A

Purpose: To develop balance and to have fun in a competitive setting

Prerequisite: None

Procedure: All of these circle games are to be played by two wrestlers at a time in a 10 – foot circle.

Cockfight: Each wrestler holds a foot off of the mat with a hand and attempts to force the other out of the circle.

Ankle Grab: Each wrestler bends over, grabs his own ankles, and then attempts to bump the other out of the circle.

Single Leg Bump: Each wrestler raises his right leg off the mat, folds his arms in front of himself, and tries to force the other off of the mat using only the raised leg.

Coaching Points: These circle games can be used for combative contests at the end of wrestling practice or during a physical education wrestling unit.

10.38 Knee Football

Skill Level: Junior high, senior high

Basic Skill: N/A

Purpose: To be used as an alternative to regular wrestling practice

Prerequisite: None

Procedure: This game is played in a wrestling room with the walls serving as the out-of-bounds lines. Goal lines are drawn with tape at both ends of the room. The wrestlers are divided into two teams, and rules are similar to regular football rules except all players are on their knees. A team has four downs to make a touchdown or first down. First downs are accomplished by completing two passes beyond the line of scrimmage. Teams may run only once every four downs. No participant may stand on his feet (this limits contact to low-impact wrestling-like contact). Teams must announce their intentions on the fourth down: punt or go for a score. The ball is thrown for kickoffs and punts. It is legal to catch balls off the walls. A regular football, nerf-ball, or taped towel may be used for the ball.

Safety Concerns: Insist that all action stop on the whistle, to cut down the chance of injury (even though the chance is minimal because most contact is low-impact). The smaller wrestlers will have a tendency to avoid piling up or going head up with the heavyweights.

10.39 Snake

Skill Level: Peewee

Basic Skill: N/A

Purpose: To simulate the crawl position a wrestler might use to regain his base in the down position

Prerequisite: None

Procedure: Wrestlers are instructed to stay within the confines of the large wrestling circle. One wrestler is designated as the snake; he slithers around on his belly attempting to tag the other wrestlers, who are running about on their feet. As a wrestler is tapped, he too becomes a snake. This continues until only one wrestler is left standing. He is declared the winner and will be the snake for the start of the next game.

Coaching Points: You may wish to modify this contest and play Squirrel instead, which is the same game except that wrestlers are allowed to move on their hands and knees instead of on their bellies.

10.40 Duck Duck Goose

Skill Level: Peewee, junior high

Basic Skill: N/A

Purpose: To provide simple fun for elementary and middle school wrestlers on the wrestling mat

Prerequisite: None

Procedure: All but one of the wrestlers sit Indian style in a circle; they are ducks. The other wrestler is the goose and walks around the outside of the circle tapping the heads of the sitting wrestlers. Each time the goose taps a head he will say "Duck." To challenge a certain wrestler for his spot on the mat, he says "Goose." Immediately both wrestlers run around the circle to reach the vacated spot on the mat. If the duck can catch the goose and tap him, he gets to sit back in his spot. If the duck does not tap the goose, he becomes the goose for the next round.

Coaching Points: This should only be use for elementary or middle school children in a wrestling practice room or in a physical education setting.

10.41 Thumb Wrestling

Skill Level: Peewee

Basic Skill: N/A

Purpose: To develop fine motor skills and to get youngsters thinking about wrestling

Prerequisite: None

Procedure: The opponents lock their right hands using a chin grip (fingers only). They then tap their thumbs together three times. The contest begins after the third tap. The object is to pin the thumb of the opponent to the top of the index finer, which serves as the mat. Instruct the combatants that to score a pin they must count "1,001, 1,002, 1,003" and not "1, 2, 3" as in the media-pro wrestling.

Coaching Points: Children can imagine themselves as Greco-Roman wrestlers, going out to win with brute strength, or slick, baiting their opponents by laying their thumbs near a pin position only to duck out for a pin of their own at the last second. A "just for fun" activity.

10.42 Knock Down

Skill Level: Peewee, junior high, senior high

Basic Skill: N/A

Purpose: To have fun on a wrestling mat and to provide a weight reduction workout

Prerequisite: None

Procedure: The wrestlers are in a wrestling room with a nerf soccer ball or nerf volleyball. The object of the game is to "knock down" (hit) each of the other wrestlers in the room. The last man standing is the champion. The game begins with the coach throwing the ball into the air. The wrestler who catches the ball is allowed to take a maximum of three steps in trying to hit another wrestler with the ball. A wrestler who has been "knocked down" may get back up if he gets the ball back. However, a downed man is not allowed to move around the get a loose ball; he must instead intercept a thrown or rolling ball.

Coaching Points: The wrestlers are constantly moving during this game, and it is a fun activity that can be used for losing weight. This game can be played in teams.

10.43 Vision Quest

Skill Level: Junior high, senior high

Basic Skill: N/A

Purpose: To be used for a "psych" session before dual meets or tournaments

Prerequisite: None

Procedure: All wrestlers on the team form a big circle and lie belly down. They pound on the mat, and if the coach desires, chant "Beat Smithfield" or whomever the next opponent happens to be. As the team pounds on the mat, one wrestler stand up and runs around the circle, stepping in between each wrestler beside him does the same thing. Each wrestler rounds the circle, and then the coach gives his goal-oriented psychological speech for the upcoming match.

Coaching Points: This exercise is mainly for ritual situations. It's of limited benefit for actual wrestling training or competition.

Chapter 11

WARM-UP AND CONDITIONING ACTIVITIES

The activities in this chapter explore exercises that can be utilized to warm up the wrestler, build endurance, increase flexibility, and help maintain strength during the season. Weight lifting is not specifically discussed here due to the many weight training resources currently on the market. However, most successful wrestling programs do include some type of weight training as a part of the training regime.

The chapter begins with an explanation of a variety of warm-up methods that coaches have successfully implemented. This is followed by description of a pre-season conditioning camp and a variety of other conditioning activities.

The exercises in this chapter can be valuable aids for the coach who wishes to add variety to the warm up and conditioning portions of their program.

CHAPTER INDEX

11.1 International Team Warm-Up

Skill Level: Peewee, junior high, senior high, college

Basic Skill: Position, motion, level change, penetration

Purpose: To increase blood flow and elevate body temperature before stretching exercises and actual practice

Prerequisite: None

Procedure: The captain leads the other wrestlers around the wrestling room in single file, jogging, the wrestlers mirroring the captain's movements. Many motor activities can be mixed in with the jogging, including penetration steps, two-leg hops, one-leg hops, skipping, cartwheels, somersaults, shoulder rolls, backward running, carioca, handsprings, headsprings, "walking like an Egyptian," seal walks, hand-foot taps, and buddy-carries. This warm-up activity should take about 8-12 minutes.

Coaching Points: It is enjoyable to rotate leaders and to have each wrestler come up with other creative motor activities. Coaches may wish to play music or have the wrestlers sing as they exercise.

Safety Concerns: Do not select gymnastics stunts such as back flips or handsprings for any group that has not had prior experience in executing those types of skills.

11.2 Ladder Workout NEW

Skill Level: Peewee, junior high, senior high, college

Purpose: To use as a warm-up activity or conditioning acativity and to increase basic foot speed.

Prerequisite: None

Procedure: Coaches may purchase a commercial ladder or simply use colored mat tape to tape a ladder on the mat *(figure A)*. This drill can be incorporated into the warm ups and coaches may dictate the various steps to be completed. There are a variety exercises documented in texts and on the internet.

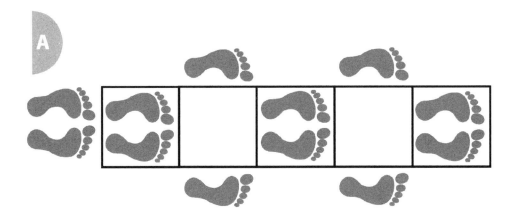

11.3 A 10-Day Preseason Conditioning Camp
(formerly used at Brandon, FL High School)

Skill Level: Junior high, senior high, college

Purpose: To improve cardio respiratory function and the condition of various muscle groups essential for wrestling, to provide a symbol of physical excellence, and to give wrestlers a feeling of team unity

Prerequisite: The wrestlers should have participated in a basic weight training or conditioning program before beginning the 10-day program.

Procedure: The camp is held just before the beginning of the season, and all students in the school setting are encouraged to participate.

It runs for three weeks, beginning on a Wednesday and continuing on the following schedule: Thursday, Monday, Tuesday, Wednesday, Thursday, Monday, Tuesday and Wednesday, then ending with various competitions on Thursday (Day 10). No workouts are scheduled for Fridays or the weekends due to football season. All participants who complete every one of each day's scheduled exercises are presented with a t-shirt signifying their accomplishment. Participants who win the various contests are presented with wrestling memorabilia, such as wrestling posters or wrestling belt buckles.

The following paragraphs describe the basic daily workout and are followed by a chart that lists the entire 10-day cycle. The workout begins outside each day with the wrestlers doing three sets of pull-ups (maxing on each set), and three sets of push-ups (maximum for 1-minute time period), and three sets of sit-ups (maximum for 1-minute time period). The wrestlers use three different grips for the pull-ups: palms away, palms forward, and baseball grip.

The wrestlers then do a timed run varying in distance from 1.4 to 3.5 miles and return to the wrestling room. Once the workout has moved indoors, the wrestlers complete a circuit training exercise routing consisting of neck work, handstand push-ups, buddy's (inverted sit-ups), pummeling, lift drills, arching drills, jumping rope, climbing rope, and jump squats. Each wrestler goes through the circuit three times, and each time the amount of exercises to be performed changes. For instance, the inverted push-ups are done for 15 repetitions the first time, maxing to total fatigue the second time, and then 10 repetitions the third time. The times and amount also change over the 10-day period.

The following are brief explanation of each exercise:

Neck Work: The three neck exercises used in this circuit are 9.16 Bridge-Around-High Leg Drill, 11.10 Pullover Bridge with a partner, and bridging with a partner sitting on the thighs *(figure A)*.

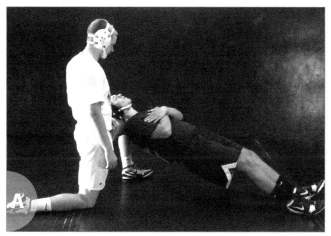

Buddy's: The inverted sit-up is executed by the light wrestler lying flat on the mat in a belly-up position. He does the sit-ups after proper position has been attained. The dark wrestler steps between the light wrestler's legs, bends over, and locks around his own knees. He then picks the light wrestler up, forming a horizontal surface underneath the light wrestler's buttocks with his knees. The light wrestler is now in position for sit-ups (*figure B*).

Handstand Push-Ups: A partner holds the legs for balance (*figure C*).

Arching Drills: The arching drills consist of bridging from the knees (sitting on the knees and leaning back into a back bridge), 5.7 Hand-Walk the Wall back arch, walking on the hands (with help if needed) and the 5.9 Hand Grip-Back Arch

Jumping Rope: The wrestlers skip rope for a prescribed time period

Pummeling: (see 5.3 Pummeling Drill)

Lift Drills: (see 5.1 Lift Drill)

Climbing Rope: *The wrestlers climb a rope*: **A–** without using their legs, **B–** using their legs, and **C–** Donkey Kong style: two ropes at the same time, one arm on each rope.

Jump Squats: The wrestlers put their hands on their heads and repeatedly jump up in the air and down into a low squat position.

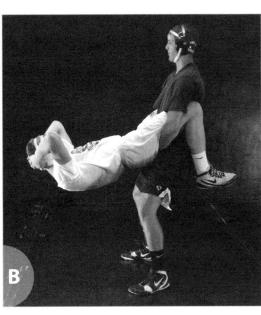

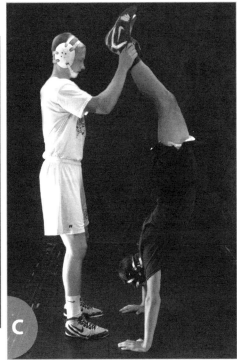

The daily workouts conclude with several sprints approximately the length of the gym. The coach evaluates the day's work while the wrestlers rest in squat positions, leaning against the wall. On day 8 the wrestlers participate in a 2-mile buddy carry, carrying each other for a 2-mile time distance run, switching roles whenever fatigue dictates. Day 9 includes a 3.5 mile timed run. Day 10 consists of a chin-up contest, a 6-mile timed run, and a baseball game. The boys are divided into two teams for the Day 10 activities; usually it's varsity versus the new kids, with the winning team awarded fruit drinks and fruits immediately following the half-hour baseball game.

Coaching Points: You might have participants get a physical examination before they start this workout. This is an excellent preseason conditioning routine because it not only stresses cardiovascular endurance but also begins toning muscles and includes muscle movements that will be needed for the upcoming wrestling season. The daily workout last approximately 2 hours, and you should record all exercises requiring timing or a maximum output so you can pick out the champions in each event.

Brandon Workout					
Activity	Day 1 Wednesday	Day 2 Thursday	Day 3 Monday	Day 4 Tuesday	Day 5 Wednesday
Max Pulls 3x					
Max Push-ups 3x	1 minute per set each day				
Max Sit-ups 3x					
Neck Isometrics	:30	:45	:45	1:00	1:00
Run	1.4 miles	3 mi.	Same	3.5 mi	1.4 fast
Neck	3 Sets (1-5) 1 – Flip Spin 2 – Kick over 3 – Sit on thighs	Same each day			
Handstand push-ups	15/max 1 min/10	Same	2 set/max 1 easy	2 max/ 1 hands touch	Max/Max/10
Buddy's	10/max 1 min/10	Same	2 set max/ 1 easy	2 max/use hands/fast	Max/max/10
Pummel	:30/:30/100	:45/:30/:45	1 min	1:15/:45/120 count	1:00/100 count/1:15
Lifting	6 doubles/ single leg ducks	Fire 3x	3x double	3x /10 each	15/6/12
Neck	6-10 bridge on knee/walk wall/walk on hands/ hand grip-back arch each day				
Rope jump	1:15/:30/1:20	1:00/3x	3x/1:00	1:15/:30/1:20	1:00/:30/1:30
Ropes	Fast/no leg/ Donkey Kong	Same each day			
Squat jumps	10 – 3 sets	11 – 3 sets	12 – 3 sets	14 – 3 sets	15 – 3 sets
Sprints	4 sprints and sit on wall/2 min	4-8 2:00	4-8 2:00	4-8 2:00	7-8 2:30

Brandon Workout				
Activity	Day 6 Thursday	Day 7 Monday	Day 8 Tuesday	Day 9 Wednesday
Max Pulls 3x				
Max Push-ups 3x		1 minute per set each day		
Max Sit-ups 3x				
Neck Isometrics	1:15	1:30	1:45	2:00
Run	3 miles hard	3.5 mi.	2 mi. buddy carry	2 mi.
Neck	3 Sets (1-5) 1 – Flip Spin 2 – Kick over 3 – Sit on thighs	Same each day		
Handstand push-ups	Max/max/ hands touch	Max/20/18	Max/max hands together	Same
Buddy's	max/max/use	Max/15/10	Max/max hands behind head	Same
Pummel	:30/:30/100	1:30/100 count/1:15	1:45/100 count/1:30	Same
Lifting	6 doubles/ single leg ducks each day			
Neck	6-10 bridge on knee/walk wall/walk on hands/hand grip-back arch each day			
Rope jump	1:15/:30 fast/2:00	1:30/:45 fast/2:00	1:30/:45 fast/2:00	2:00/:45/2:00
Ropes	Fast/no leg/ Donkey Kong	Same each day		
Squat jumps	16 – 3 sets	17 – 3 sets	18 – 3 sets	19 – 3 sets
Sprints	4 sprints and sit on wall/2 min	4-8 3:00	4-8 3:00	4-8 3:00

Day 10 – Thursday
Fun and Celebration!

Teams: Chin-up contest; 6 – mi. run; Baseball game

To Classroom for Awards:

1st) Shirt presentations

2nd) Winning Team: Fruit and/or fruit juice

3rd) Mr. Exercise Award

11.4 The Ready Sandbag Workout

Skill Level: Junior high, senior high, college

Purpose: To provide a cardiovascular workout with equal muscular-endurance and strength-maintenance benefits

Prerequisite: None

Procedure: This drill is known as a 12-by-12 workout. There are 12 exercises, and each is to be performed for 12 repetitions. Following completion of an exercise, a wrestler moves immediately to the next exercise without resting, thus allowing for a positive cardiovascular effect.

Back Bridge: The wrestler gets into a back bridge and holds the sandbag on his chest, pressing it until his arms are completely extended *(figure A)*. The motion is similar to a bench press and should be done 12 times.

Hack Squat: The wrestler stands, holding the sandbag between his legs. He grasps the bag with one hand in front of his legs and one hand behind his legs, and then performs 12 regular squats *(figure B)*.

Triceps Extension: The wrestler holds the bag behind his head while in a standing position *(figure C)*. He presses the bag in a manner similar to a French curl 12 times.

Regular Squat: The wrestler holds the bag on his shoulder and performs 12 regular squats.

Upright Row: The wrestler spreads his legs and bends over, forming a 120-degree angle at the waist, keeping his back parallel to the floor, and then lifts the bag to his chest 12 times.

Back Squats: The wrestler holds the bag behind his buttocks and completes 12 squats.

Zimmers: The wrestler does 12 jump squats while holding the bag to his chest.

Bent Rows: This is the same as upright rows except the wrestler is bent over to a 90-degree angle at the waist.

Calf-Raises: The wrestler holds the bag on his shoulders and raises up on his toes for 12 repetitions.

Front Press: This is a regular military press using the bag and pressing it overhead for 12 repetitions.

Biceps Curls: This exercise consists of curling the sandbag for 12 repetitions.

Coaching Points: This routine is very beneficial as a total body workout. It affects almost every muscle group in the body and promotes cardiovascular development. The routine can be completed in a very short period of time. Use differently weighted bags for the various weight classes. For example, use 25-pound bags for lightweights, 35-pound bags for middleweights, and 45-pound bags for heavyweights.

Safety Concerns: If sandbags are used at the junior high level, make sure wrestlers have been instructed in basic weight training principles and movements.

11.5 PTA (Pain, Torture, Agony)

Skill Level: Junior high, senior high, college

Purpose: To engage in a series of high intensity wrestling-related activities to push beyond the normal range of mental and physical fatigue, thus allowing for maximum physical performance in a competitive setting

Prerequisite: The wrestlers must be able to perform basic wrestling exercises and maneuvers.

Procedure: The wrestlers are instructed that they will engage in a series of physical activities involving constant motion for a given time period, usually 8 to 15 minutes. They are informed that no matter how tired they may feel, their bodies have the physical ability to continue to perform. (The PTA routine is a mind-over-matter exercise designed to develop mental toughness.)

Because these routines include numerous buddy exercises, wrestlers should choose partners. A coach may incorporate any activity into the PTA routine and should vary the activities depending upon the effects desired. Listed here are two samples of 10-minute PTA routines; the first incorporates mostly wrestling skills, and the second is designed specifically for physical endurance.

Routine 1	Routine 2
Wrestling Skill PTA	**Physical Endurance PTA**
1 Snaps and spins	1 Run in place
2 Snap-spin and Hip drag	2 Hop to ceiling
3 Floating	3 Wheelbarrow push-ups
4 Shoot and Leap frog	4 Grass drills
5 Penetration Shots	5 Sit-out and roll-even
6 Double-ups	6 Buddy carries around room
7 Run in place and sprawl	7 Push-ups
8 Pummel	8 Buddy hops (hop over partner in referee's position
9 Spinning	9 Buddy Squats
10 Body lifts	10 Squat thrusts

Unless otherwise stated, each wrestler performs the exercise for 30 seconds.

Coaching Points: You might want to combine activities from each routine to form a third routine to emphasize the performance of simple wrestling skills while the wrestler's bodies are fatigued. To obtain maximum physical benefits, the PTA routine should be held toward the end of practice so that the wrestlers' heart rates will already be elevated.

11.6 Ike Iron Workout **NEW**

Skill Level: Junior high, senior high, college

Purpose: This workout allows wrestlers to maintain upper body strength throughout the season.

Prerequisite: Wrestlers should posses a basic knowledge of weight lifting principles. There needs to be two dumbbells of varying weights in an area close to the practice mat and near the team's pull-up bars.

Procedure: Coaches will number each set of wrestling partners at the beginning of practice; for example 1-20 if there are 40 wrestlers in the room.

During the drill phase of practice, the wrestlers will go four at a time to the dumbbell area and complete the following:

- **10 Bicep Curls**
- **10 Military Presses**
- **10 Rows**
- **10 Pull-Ups**

Once they complete the exercises they will call out the next highest number and four more wrestlers go to the workout. Wrestlers typically will get to the weight station 3-4 times during a practice.

Coaching Points: This is an excellent conditioning exercise for maintaining upper body strength. Also, because the area is near the mat, the wrestlers can be mentally practicing the drills that are being completed in the practice setting. Encourage wrestlers to push themselves!

11.7 Mat Pull-Ups

Skill Level: Junior high, senior high, college

Purpose: This exercise allows wrestlers to do pull-ups even when no pulling bar is available in the wrestling room

Prerequisite: None

Procedure: One wrestler lies flat on his back with a partner standing over him straddling his chest area. The wrestler standing lets his arms hang to his sides, raising only his forearms to form a 90-degree angle at the elbows *(figure A)*. The down man reaches up and holds on to the standing man's wrists. He must maintain a rigid position to do mat pull-ups; only his heels will be on the mat.

Coaching Points: Not only is this an excellent conditioning exercise for the down wrestler, but it also offers an isometric contraction for the arms of the standing man.

11.8 Towel Pull-Ups

Skill Level: Peewee. junior high, senior high, college

Purpose: To increase a wrestler's grip while developing the "pull" muscles needed for capturing a single leg

Prerequisite: None

Procedure: A towel should be thrown over a pull-up bar. Wrestlers execute their pull-ups while grasping each end of the hanging towel instead of using the pull-up bar *(figure A)*. Wrestlers may also use a resistance band or weighted jump rope to do pull-ups.

Coaching Points: This exercise not only increases a wrestler's grip but also more exactly duplicates a single leg attack. Encourage this type of pull-up exercise because of the multiple benefits attained.

11.9 Two-Man Sit-Ups

Skill Level: Junior high, senior high, college

Purpose: To add flexibility to the sit-up motion and allow a wrestler to exercise muscles past the normal range of motion of a regular sit-up

Prerequisite: None

Procedure: One wrestler assumes a down referee's position and his partner sits on his back. The top man faces toward the buttocks of the bottom man and hooks his feet in the bottom man's thigh region *(figure A)*. He is now ready to do sit-ups, attempting to touch his head on or near the mat with each repetition. If needed, the bottom man may use his neck to aid the top man in coming back into the upright position.

Coaching Points: You may want your wrestlers to turn belly-down in the same position and perform back hyperextension immediately following the sit-up exercise to strengthen the back muscles.

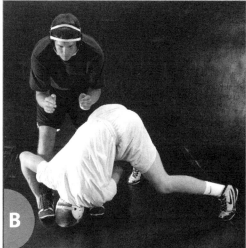

11.10 Pullover Bridge

REVISED

Skill Level: All levels

Purpose: To strengthen the neck muscles while in a bridge position and to execute movement

Prerequisite: None

Procedure: The light wrestler assumes a back bridge, extending his arms and grasping the ankles of his partner, who is standing in front of him. The light wrestler kicks over into a front bridge with his legs to the side of his partner. The light wrestler then kicks back into the back bridge position. The bridging wrestler should kick into his front bridge on both sides of his partner and finally kick straight over so that he straddles his partner's legs *(figures A,B,C)*.

Coaching Points: The wrestlers will have to pull with their arms to make this drill work at first.

11.11 Two-Man Bridge

Skill Level: Senior high, college

Purpose: To condition neck muscles that are needed for bridging when attempting to avoid a pinning situation

Prerequisite: The wrestlers should be able to bridge by themselves.

Procedure: One wrestler lies on his back and moves into a back bridge position. His partner lies across his chest to provide added resistance *(figure A)*. After the wrestlers have become accustomed to this type of exercise, the top man sits on the bridging wrester's thighs, placing his feet on his chest *(figure B)*. This offers added resistance.

Coaching Points: This drill can be expanded to include a live combat scenario, in which the top wrestler applies a half-nelson–crotch combination. The bottom wrestler, on the coach's signal, attempts to bridge and escape from the pinning situation.

Safety Concerns: You must be cautious about using this exercise for younger wrestlers, due to their physical immaturity. It does provide an excellent match-like situation for the older boys who have full physical development.

11.12 Back Pullovers

Skill Level: Junior high, senior high, college

Purpose: To increase flexibility of the back muscles and to experience kinesthetic awareness of being thrown

Prerequisite: None

Procedure: Two wrestlers stand up back to back, extend their arms over their heads, and grasp hands using a finger-chain grip *(figure A)*. One wrestler bends forward, pulling his partner over his back into a standing position *(figure B)*.

Coaching Points: This drill should be performed before using back arch maneuvers.

11.13 Head Lift Drill

Skill Level: Senior high, college

Purpose: To lift an opponent from the mat using only the head for support

Prerequisite: The wrestlers should have performed numerous neck-strengthening and flexibility exercises.

Procedure: The dark wrestler assumes a one-knee-up, one-knee-down position; the light wrestler leans over dark's head. On command, the dark wrestler comes to his feet, lifting light into the air, using only his head for support and balance *(figure A)*.

Coaching Points: Inform the wrestlers that in certain situations they will have to use their heads to lift or drive an opponent.

Safety Concerns: Wrestlers should perform exercise routines designed to strengthen the neck muscles before attempting this type of lift. In any case, make sure that the wrestlers have completed exercises before attempting this skill.

11.14 Body Row

Skill Level: Senior high, college

Purpose: To be used as a rowing exercise when weights are not available

Prerequisite: None

Procedure: The wrestlers start in a standing belly-to-back position with one wrestler attaining a rear standing body lock position. The rear man lifts his partner from the mat and lowers him between his legs. The partner must maintain a perfectly rigid position (in other words, he must keep his body straight). After the rear man has lowered his partner between his legs, he lifts him back to a standing position. The next time he bends over, lowering his partner to the side, returns to the upright position, and finally lowers his partner to the other side *(figure A)*. This routine should be repeated several times.

Coaching Points: This is an excellent exercise for developing lower back muscles. It is also an excellent exercise for training individuals for Freestyle and Greco-Roman wrestling techniques, because some of those situations dictate lifting a wrestler from the mat.

11.15 Body Curl

Skill Level: Senior high, college

Purpose: To allow wrestlers to execute a curling-type exercise without using a barbell or weights, and to work on a basic hip thrust. This is an important skill for lifting or arching.

Prerequisite: The wrestlers should be able to curl using a barbell.

Procedure: One wrestler stands and his partner jumps into his arms as if he were a baby. The wrestler holding the "baby" then uses his arms to curl the body. If the partner is too heavy to do a perfect curl, allow the wrestler to "cheat with his hips." The cheating motion creates a hip thrust; this skill is helpful for lifting, arching and blocking penetration shots. However, if hip power is not desired, don't allow the wrestlers to cheat with their hips *(figure A)*.

Coaching Points: You must realize that to develop maximum strength in the biceps area, the hips should not be used. However, hip power and movement are integral parts of wrestling, so the hip thrust provides some positive benefits.

11.16 Monkey Roll Contest

Skill Level: Junior high, senior high

Purpose: To enhance a wrestler's ability to scramble on the mat

Prerequisite: None

Procedure: Three wrestlers lie belly-down. The wrestler on the right jumps over the middle wrestler, hits belly-down, and rolls under the wrestler on the left. The middle wrestler rolls to the right and repeats the same steps. The wrestler on the left has hopped over the first wrestler and rolled under the second wrestler, and now he stands and begins the same routine. The contest is to see how many times the first wrestler goes completely through the cycle.

Coaching Points: The monkey rolls can also be used as an agility drill for everyday practice.

11.17 Shoot and Leap Frog

Skill Level: Junior high, senior high, college

Purpose: To be part of circuit training exercise and used as a penetration drill

Prerequisite: The wrestlers must be able to execute penetration

Procedure: One wrestler simulates a low single penetration as he shoots between his partner's legs *(figure A)*. Immediately following his shot, he stands and leaps back over his partner's back *(figure B)*. The entire routine continues for a certain time period. Roles are reversed for the next time session.

Coaching Points: Be careful that the low single shots do not become an "overextended dive through." The overextension is a bad habit that may carry over into a match situation. Overextension during penetration may allow an opponent to score a takedown using a snap down maneuver. This drill is also known as going "in and out of the window."

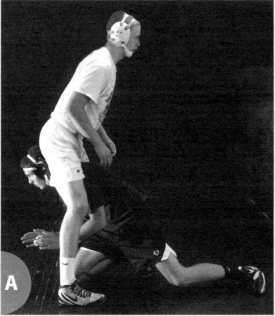

11.18 Partner Dive-Over

Skill Level: Peewee. junior high, senior high

Purpose: To increase flexibility of the muscles in the lower back area

Prerequisite: None

Procedure: One wrestler assumes a down referee's position. His partner stands beside him, bends over, and grasps onto his neck and stomach area. He then executes a forward roll *(figure A)*, maintaining is grip so that he ends up in a back arch position with his head under his partner's stomach. He then kicks back into the starting position and repeats the exercise.

Coaching Points: The bottom man must assume a sturdy base for the exercise for be successful.

11.19 Hand Grip

Skill Level: Junior high, senior high, college

Purpose: To develop a strong hand grip

Prerequisite: None

Procedure: A wrestler can increase the strength of his hand grip by squeezing a tennis ball or a piece of the mat. Pieces of scrap mat can be cut to fit a wrestler's hand and can be carried in a jacket pocket. The wrestler should squeeze the ball or mat for at least 10 seconds per repetition. Unlimited repetitions may be performed.

Coaching Points: This is an exercise wrestlers can perform on the bus, at lunchtime, or just walking down the hall at school.

11.20 Chair Carry NEW

Skill Level: Junior high, senior high, college

Purpose: To develop a strong hand grip, leg strength/endurance and general cardio conditioning.

Prerequisite: None

Procedure: Groups of three. One wrestler sits in a chair while two others carry the chair. Object is to cover the length of the mat three times. Each time you cover the length of the mat a different person is on the chair.

Coaching Points: This is an exercise wrestlers can perform any time during practice to break up the routine of practice or it can be used strictly during the conditioning portion of practice.

11.21 Resistance Band Drills (Conditioning specific) **NEW**

Skill Level: Junior high, senior high, college

Purpose: To maintain strength and flexibility throughout the season

Prerequisite: Basic knowledge of weight lifting procedures

Procedure: Coaches may wish to have wrestlers complete the basic muscle group exercises such as bicep curls, triceps curls *(figure A)*, rows *(figure B)*, squats, and so on as part of the conditioning portion of practice.

Coaching Points: This is an exercise wrestlers can perform any time during practice to break up the routine of practice or it can be used strictly during the conditioning portion of practice.

11.22 Resistance Band Drills (Wrestling specific) NEW

Skill Level: Junior high, senior high, college

Purpose: To maintain strength and flexibility throughout the season

Prerequisite: Basic knowledge of weight lifting procedures

Procedure: Coaches may wish to have wrestlers complete exercises that are specific to wrestling. Wrestlers can execute these drills with a partner holding the resistance band or by attaching it to a stationary object such as a pull-up bar.

Figure A shows the light wrestler doing penetration steps with his partner holding the band.

Figure B shows how a wrestler might use a pull-up bar to hold the band while he practices a snap down action. The resistance band may also be used to do bicep curls, tricep curls, rows, squats, etc., as part of the conditioning portion of practice.

Coaching Points: These are exercises that wrestlers can perform any time during practice. They can be used to break up the monotony of practice or they can be used strictly during the conditioning portion of practice.

Safety Points: Inform wrestlers that if they are using a stationary object to use the resistance bands that they **DO NOT** tie one end to the object, but rather loop it around the object and hold both ends of the band. Bands that are tied at one end may come lose and snap into the wrestler causing injury.

11.23 Carpet Runs **NEW**

Skill Level: Junior high, senior high, college

Purpose: To develop core strength, leg strength, endurance and general cardio conditioning.

Prerequisite: None

Procedure: Wrestlers will push a carpet square (*figure A*) down a hallway (20-50 meters) or on the mat. Coaches may have the wrestlers complete another exercise such a buddy squats or standing wrestling drills at the end or the hallway for recovery between runs.

Coaching Points: This is an exercise wrestlers can perform any time during practice to break up the routine of practice or it can be used strictly during the conditioning portion of practice.

CAUTION: Also, be sure that the hallway surface is smooth and that there are no obstacles in the pathway. Especially note doors that may open into the path or adjoining hallways where pedestrian may cross into the pathway of the wrestlers.

11.24 Ironhower Medicine Ball Workouts NEW

Skill Level: Junior high, senior high, college

Purpose: To develop core strength, leg strength, endurance, general cardio conditioning and overall mental toughness.

Prerequisite: None

Procedure: This is an activity that can be used during practice to develop general overall wrestling-specific conditioning and mental toughness. It might be best used as a conditioning activity to conclude practice. This medicine ball workout is completed with a partner and includes 10 activities to be completed for a specific time period (coaches might determine a 30 seconds to one minute time period per activity depending on the type of workout).

Coaching Points: This is an exercise wrestlers can perform any time during practice to break up the routine of practice or it can be used strictly during the conditioning portion of practice. Also, be sure that the wrestlers have a clear understanding of each exercise before going full speed. Coaches will inform the team what exercise is to be completed and keep time for partner switches within each exercise if needed.

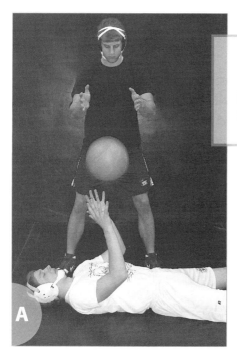

1 **Blasters**-This is a traditional activity with one wrestler laying on his back and pushing the ball to a partner *(figure A)*.

2 **Back to Back**-Partners pass the ball to one another over their shoulder *(figure A)*. They should alternate shoulders after 30 seconds.

3 **Sit-ups-**Partners lock their ankles and pass the ball to one another while completing sit-ups. Note that the ball is extended over head on the down portion of the sit-up *(figure A)*. An alternate form for this drill is to have the wrestler doing the sit-ups to throw the ball to a standing wrestler *(figure B)* (Coaches could have the standing wrestler execute a sprawl to the mat and back to their feet before the light wrestler throws the ball back.)

4 **Stance to Wall-**One wrestler pushes the ball to the wall and catches it using a side to side and forward motion. Each wrestler will complete the exercise for 15 seconds and alternate with his partner *(figure A)*. The other wrestler recovers using an active rest (e.g., jumping, shuffling, jogging in place or pretend jumping rope).

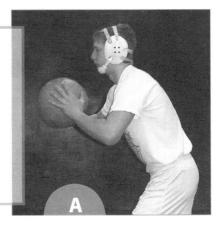

5A **Pushups-**The light wrestler executes pushups by using a triangle hand formation on the ball *(figure A)* or by mountain climbing over the ball (one hand on the mat and one hand on the ball) *(figure B and C)*. The light wrestler completes hops over the wrestler's legs *(figure D)*. Wrestlers change positions after a prescribed time period.

5B **Pushup Alternative-** Wrestler can do pushups while partner holds the ball on his neck *(figure E)*. Alternate every 15-30 seconds.

6 **Sprawl Drill-**The light wrestler chest passes the ball to the dark wrestler *(figure A)* and then completes a hip down sprawl *(figure B)* and circles back to feet *(figure C)* before the light passes the ball back to him. Roles are reversed after 30 seconds. **CAUTION: Coaches should make sure that there is plenty of room for all wrestlers to execute the sprawls without kicking someone. Also, advise the wrestlers throwing the ball to make sure their partner is ready to receive the pass.**

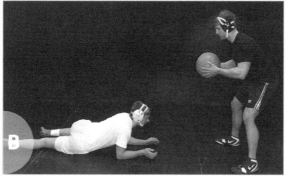

7 **Walking lunges-**Wrestler walks the length of the room with medicine ball completing lunges *(figure D)*. The partner recovers using some form of active (e.g., jumping, shuffling, jogging in place or pretend jumping rope).

8 Standup Drill-Wrestler gets into a down referee's position and a ball is placed on the neck area by a partner *(figure A)*. Wrestler pushes up and back (simulating a standup) throwing ball off the neck area and into his partners grasp *(figure B)*.

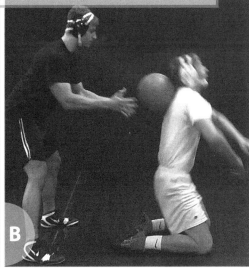

9 Wall Squat- Wrestler places the ball between himself and the wall. He then completes a 4-count (1,2,3,4) wall squat down and back up *(figure C)*.

10 Back to Back-Wrestlers pass the ball between their legs to their partner who completes a curl (i.e., bicep curl) and military press (i.e., press ball over head to full extension of the arms). Then it is passed to their partner and he completes the curl and military press.

Chapter 12

POSITION DRILLS
(For Live Wrestling)

The photos in this chapter show a variety of position scenarios a coach may want to use in a "live wrestling" setting to prepare wrestlers for actual combat in a match. The scenarios are typical positions that wrestlers often find themselves in during a competitive situation. Therefore wrestlers should be drilled to react in ways that become automatic when the position arises.

   The following pages include a variety of positions in which wrestlers will often find themselves during competition. These are examples of positions with which coaches might want their wrestlers to become familiar. All of the positions in the following situations can and should be adjusted during practice sessions.

   Authors Note: *Since the first edition of this book, wrestlers have become extremely adept at countering offensive takedowns. In the past, wrestlers countered offensive shots by sprawling and then using an old fashioned cross face or hip drag to counter score. However, with offensive setups and penetration shots becoming so good, wrestlers get so deep on shots that the defensive wrestlers have countered by coming over the top and locking on the waist, crotch, or on legs. The term that has evolved for these defensive maneuvers is "funk." Interviews with a number of high level coaches indicated that the "funk" is relatively hard to drill (and that is why there are no funk drills in the feet chapter). Coaches suggested that the wrestlers practice the "funk" from position live wrestling scenarios to develop a feel for the action.*

CHAPTER INDEX ALL NEW

NEUTRAL POSITION SCENARIOS

12.1 On double not locked

12.2 On double ready to drive

12.3 On double -1/2 sprawl

Head in middle

Double off mat

12.4 On single-extended

12.5 On single-turning corner

12.6 On single-leg up

12.7 Body lock

12.8 Headlock standing

12.9 Russian Tie

12.10 Duck under position

12.11 Funk 1

12.12 Funk 2

12.13 Funk 3

12.14 Funk 4

TOP AND BOTTOM SCENARIOS

12.15 Half nelson on side going to back

12.16 Legs-in on knees

12.17 Legs-in on side

12.18 Legs-in high half

12.19 High half on knees

12.20 High half on hip

12.21 Two on one (flat)

12.22 One on one (flat)

12.23 Standing rear position

12.24 Crab ride

12.25 Tilt position

12.26 Sit back position

12.27 Caught in a headlock

12.28 Near-side cradle

12.29 Far-side cradle

Chapter **13**

SITUATION DRILLS
(For Live Wrestling)

The drills in this chapter lists a variety of situations that a coach may want to use to prepare wrestlers for those "just in case" moments during a match. Most of these situations occur toward the end of a period or a match when there is not a lot of time for decision-making on the part of the wrestler. Therefore wrestlers should be drilled to react in ways that become automatic when the situation arises.

  The following pages include a variety of situations in which wrestlers will find themselves during competition. These are just a few examples of the situations with which coaches might want their wrestlers to be familiar. All of the times in the following situations can and should be adjusted during practice sessions.

CHAPTER INDEX ALL NEW

13.1 Top Man Situation Live Drills

Top Man in control on mat and ***winning*** in score
(no stalling has been called):

- ■ **Wrestler is ahead by 1** and in the advantage position on the mat with 20 seconds to go.
  - • Options: ride hard at all cost, take one stall call; give up no more than 1 point and go to overtime
- ■ **Wrestler is ahead by 2** and in the advantage position with 20 seconds to go.
  - • Options: ride hard, can take one stall call; give up 1 point and wrestle on feet
- ■ **Wrestler is ahead by 3** and in the advantage position with 20 seconds to go.
  - • Options: ride out, take a stall call or let up for 1 point and wrestle on feet (depending on match)

Top Man in control standing behind and ***winning*** in score
(no stalling has been called):

- ■ **Wrestler is ahead by 1** and in the standing advantage position with 20 seconds to go.
  - • Options: ride hard at all cost-drop to ankle and hold on; give up no more than 1 point and go to overtime
- ■ **Wrestler is ahead by 2** and in the advantage position with 20 seconds to go.
  - • Options: ride hard and take a stall call; give up 1 point and wrestle on feet
- ■ **Wrestler is ahead by 3** and in the advantage position with 20 seconds to go.
  - • Options: ride out, even take a stall call, or let up for 1 point and wrestle on feet

Top Man in control on mat and ***winning*** in score
(he has been warned for stalling):

- ■ **Wrestler is ahead by 1** and in the advantage position on the mat with 20 seconds to go.
  - • Options: ride hard at all cost, don't stall; give up no more than 1 point and go to overtime
- ■ **Wrestler is ahead by 2** and in the advantage position with 20 seconds to go.
  - • Options: ride hard, can take one stall call; give up 1 point and wrestle on feet
- ■ **Wrestler is ahead by 3** and in the advantage position with 20 seconds to go.
  - • Options: ride out, can afford one stall call, or let up for 1 point and wrestle on feet (depending on match)

Top Man in control standing behind and ***winning*** in score
(he has been warned for stalling)

- ■ **Wrestler is ahead by 1** and in the standing advantage position with 20 seconds to go.
  - • Options: must return opponent to mat; release for 1 point and go to overtime; take the stall call and go to overtime

266

- **Wrestler is ahead by 2** and in the standing advantage position with 20 seconds to go.
  - Options: ride hard and take a stall call; give up 1 point and wrestle on feet
- **Wrestler is ahead by 3** and in the advantage position with 20 seconds to go.
  - Options: ride out, take a stall call, or let up for 1 point and wrestle on feet

Top Man in control standing behind and *losing* in score
(no stalling has been called):

- **Wrestler is behind by 1** and in the standing advantage position with 20 seconds to go.
  - Options: bring to mat and attempt to tilt; give up 1 point and go for a tying takedown
- **Wrestler is behind by 2** and in the advantage position with 20 seconds to go.
  - Options: bring to mat and tilt for 2 or 3 points; give up 1 point and wrestle on feet attempting a 4-or 5-point throw
- **Wrestler is behind by 3** and in the advantage position with 20 seconds to go.
  - Options: bring to mat and tilt for 3 points; give up 1 point and wrestle on feet attempting a 4-or 5-point throw
- **Wrestler is behind by 4** and in the advantage position with 20 seconds to go.
  - Options: give up 1 point and wrestle on feet attempting a 5-point throw to get to overtime

Top Man in control on mat and *losing* in score
(no stalling has been called):

- **Wrestler is losing by 1** and in the advantage position on the mat with 20 seconds to go.
  - Options: ride hard and try to tilt the opponent; give up 1 point and go for a takedown to tie and go to overtime
- **Wrestler is losing by 2** and in the advantage position with 20 seconds to go.
  - Options: ride hard and try to tilt for 2 to tie or 3 points to win; give up 1 point and wrestle on feet in an attempt to score a 4-point throw
- **Wrestler is losing by 3** and in the advantage position with 20 seconds to go.
  - Options: ride out and turn opponent for 3 points to tie and go to overtime; let up for 1 point and wrestle feet attempting a 5-point throw

Top Man in control standing behind and *losing* in score
(opponent has been warned for stalling):

- **Wrestler is behind by 1** and in the standing advantage position with 20 seconds to go.
  - Options: bring to mat and attempt to tilt; give up 1 point and go for a tying takedown
- **Wrestler is behind by 2** and in the advantage position with 20 seconds to go.
  - Options: bring to mat and tilt for 2 or 3 points; give up 1 and wrestle on feet attempting a 4-or 5-point throw

■ **Wrestler is behind by 3** and in the advantage position with 20 seconds to go.
  • Options: bring to mat and tilt for 3 points; give up 1 point and wrestle on feet attempting a 4 or 5-point throw

■ **Wrestler is behind by 4** and in the advantage position with 20 seconds to go.
  • Options: give up 1 and wrestle on feet attempting a 5-point throw to get to overtime

Top Man in control on mat and *losing* in score
(opponent has been warned for stalling):

■ **Wrestler is losing by 1** and in the advantage position on the mat with 20 seconds to go.
  • Options: ride hard and try to tilt the opponent scoring or getting a stall to tie and force overtime; give up 1 point and go for a takedown to tie and go to overtime; or get a possible combination stall call and takedown to win

■ **Wrestler is losing by 2** and in the advantage position with 20 seconds to go.
  • Options: ride hard and try to tilt for 2 to tie or 3 points to win; or a possible stall call for 1 and a tilt for 2 points to win; give up 1 point and wrestle on feet in an attempt to score a 4-point throw

■ **Wrestler is losing by 3** and in the advantage position with 20 seconds to go.
  • Options: ride out and turn opponent for 3 points to tie and go to overtime; possible stall call for 1 point and a tilt for 2 points to force overtime or 3 points for the win; let up for 1 point and wrestle feet attempting a 5-point throw

13.2 Bottom Man Situation Live Drills

Bottom Man is *winning* in score *(no stalling has been called)*:

■ **Wrestler is ahead by 1** and in the down/controlled position on the mat with 20 seconds to go.

- Options: keep moving, avoid being turned at all cost, take one stall call if necessary; give up no more than 1 point to a stall and go to overtime (avoid going to back at all cost)

■ **Wrestler is ahead by 2** and in the down/controlled position with 20 seconds to go.

- Options: keep moving, avoid being turned at all cost, take one or even two stall calls if necessary; give up no more than 1 point to a stall; if absolutely necessary-take 2 points in stall penalty points and go to overtime (avoid going to back for a 3-point. near fall at all cost)

■ **Wrestler is ahead by 3** or more points and in the down/controlled position with 20 seconds to go.

- Options: keep moving, avoid being turned to the back- can take one, two or even three stall calls if necessary (and still win by a point)

Bottom Man is *winning* in score *(stalling has been called)*:

■ **Wrestler is ahead by 1** and in the down/controlled position on the mat with 20 seconds to go.

- Options: keep moving, avoid being turned at all cost, take a 1 point penalty stall call if absolutely necessary; give up no more than 1 point to a stall call and go to overtime (avoid going to back at all cost)

■ **Wrestler is ahead by 2** and in the down/controlled position with 20 seconds to go.

- Options: keep moving, avoid being turned at all cost, take one or even two stall calls if necessary; wrestler can give up 1 point in a stall call penalty; only if absolutely necessary-take 2 points in stall penalty points and go to overtime (avoid going to back for a 3-point near fall at all cost)

■ **Wrestler is ahead by 3** or more points and in the down/controlled position with 20 seconds to go.

- Options: keep moving, avoid being turned to the back- can take one or two stall calls if necessary (and still win by a point); any more stall calls and the wrestler deserves to lose

Bottom Man is *losing* in score *(stalling has been called)*:

■ **Wrestler is losing by 1** and in the down/controlled position with 8-10 seconds to go

- Options: must get an escape-recommend using a standup and score 1 point and go to overtime; might get a stall call
- **Can attempt** a reversal for the win (lower percentage)

(If no stalling has been called-recommend going for an escape to tie and get into overtime)

■ **Wrestler is losing by 2** and in the down/controlled position with 8-10 seconds to go
  • Options: Must get an escape-recommend using a standup and score 1 point and attack on feet-try for takedown and hopefully score or get a stall call for 1 point; can attempt a reversal to tie and go to overtime (lower percentage)

(If no stalling has been called-recommend going for a reversal to tie and get into overtime)

13.3 Neutral Position Situation Live Drills

Wrestler A is *winning* in score *(no stalling has been called)*:

- **Wrestler A is ahead by 1** and in the neutral position with 20 seconds to go.
  - Options: keep moving, and stay active from a defensive mindset, take one stall call (warning) if necessary; give up no more than 1 point to a stall call and go to overtime if needed to avoid being taken down
- **Wrestler A is ahead by 2** and in the neutral position with 20 seconds to go.
  - Options: keep moving, and stay active from a defensive mindset, take one stall call (warning) and a penalty point if necessary; give up no more than 2 points to stalling calls and go to overtime if needed to avoid being taken down
- **Wrestler is ahead by 3** or more points and in the neutral position with 20 seconds to go.
  - Options: keep moving, and stay active from a defensive mindset – just avoid being taken down to the back; can take a warning and 2 points in stalling if necessary (and still win by a point)

Wrestler A is *winning* in score *(he has been warned for stalling)*:

- **Wrestler A is ahead by 1** and in the neutral position with 20 seconds to go.
  - Options: keep moving, and stay active from a defensive mindset, fake offensive shots; if necessary give up 1 point to a stall call and go to overtime if needed to avoid being taken down
- **Wrestler A is ahead by 2** and in the neutral position with 20 seconds to go.
  - Options: keep moving, and stay active from a defensive mindset, take one stall call and a penalty point if necessary; worst case scenario, give up a takedown and go to overtime
- **Wrestler is ahead by 3** or more points and in the neutral position with 20 seconds to go.
  - Options: keep moving, and stay active from a defensive mindset – can actually give up a takedown, must avoid being taken down to the back; can also take two points in stalling if necessary (and still win by a point)

Wrestler A is *losing* in score *(he has been warned for stalling)*:

- **Wrestler A is losing by 1** and in the neutral position with 20 seconds to go.
  - Options: keep attacking, and fake offensive shots; try to capture a takedown to win or get a penalty point via the stall call to go to overtime
- **Wrestler A is losing by 2** and in the neutral position with 20 seconds to go.
  - Options: keep attacking, and try to capture a takedown to get into overtime; probably not enough time to get 2 penalty points via the stall calls to go to overtime

■ **Wrestler is losing by 3** or more points and in the neutral position with 20 seconds to go.

- Options: keep attacking and hope for a stall call then try to capture a takedown to go into overtime
- **Keep attacking to score** a takedown, then release and score again
- **Work for a "home run"** move (headlock, bear hug, etc.) for 4 or 5 points to win the match; probably not enough time to get two penalty points via the stall calls to go to overtime.

Overtime Situations

Overtime rules change over the years. However, in most year's one of the criteria calls for one wrestle to be put down and one wrestler to be put on top for a 30-second period. The winner is the wrestler who either gets out from the bottom position or who rides out the opponent. Therefore wrestlers should compete in an up-down referee's position and live go's throughout the season.

REFERENCES

Chapman, M. (2005). *Wrestling Tough: Dominate mentally on the mat.*
   Champaign, IL: Human Kinetics

Caslow, D. (2010, April). *Mental Toughness*: An essential wrestling ingredient.
   Pennsylvania Wrestling Newsmagazine. Retrieved from
   http://www.gobanana.com/pwn/news/mental_toughness.htm

Gable, D. (1999). *Coaching Wrestling Successfully.* Champaign, IL: Human Kinetics.

Johnson, D.A. (1991). *The Wrestling Drill Book.* Champaign, IL: Human Kinetics

Martens, R. (2004). *Successful Coaching.* Champaign, IL: Human Kinetics.

Orlick, T. (1990). *In Pursuit of Excellence.* Champaign, IL: Human Kinetics

Orlick, T. (2011). *Positive Living Skills; Joy and focus for everyone.* Renfrew,
   Ontario, Canada; General store Publishing House.

Riley, P. (1993). *The winner within: A life plan for team players.* New York, NY: The Berkley
   Publishing Group.

Weinberg, R.S. & Gould, D. (2011). *Foundations of Sports and Exercise.* Psychology.
   Champaign, IL; Human Kinetics

SPECIAL NOTE

L to R: Michael Jaskolka, Colter Johnson, Tyler Stufflebeam

A special note of thanks goes out to the three Warren County, Pennsylvania, wrestlers who served as the models for this text. Their work was strictly voluntary and none received any sort of compensation for their many hours of work. Thanks Guys!

ABOUT THE AUTHOR

Dennis A. Johnson, Ed.D.
Associate Professor School of Sport Sciences
Wingate University, Wingate, NC
djohnson@wingate.edu

Dr. Dennis A. Johnson has been involved with wrestling for over 40 years as a competitor, coach, camp director, and author. A NCAA Division I college wrestler at Marshall University, he went on to become a USA Wrestling Bronze Level certified coach and coached high school wrestling in Pennsylvania for 23 years. Dr. Johnson is co-author of *The Coaches' Guide to Nutrition and Weight Control* (first edition) and author of the first edition of *The Wrestling Drill Book* (Human Kinetics, 1991).

Currently Dr. Johnson serves as an associate professor in the School of Sport Sciences at Wingate University in Wingate, North Carolina. His academic focus centers on the psycho-social aspects of coaching and his philosophy of "athlete first-winning second" mirrors that of the American Sport Education Program. Dr. Johnson has made a number of presentations regarding mental skills training (the focus of Chapters 2 and 3) and coaching ethics in the local, regional, and national arenas. He also is the head coach for the Wingate University Division II men and women's cross country teams, qualifying for the NCAA Division II meet in 2004 and 2007.

Larry Lauer, Ph.D. CC-AASP
Championship Performance Consulting
Lauer & Associates, Director of Coaching Education and Development
The Institute for the Study of Youth Sports, Michigan State University
lauerl@msu.edu, (517) 353-5395 office

Dr. Larry Lauer is the Director of Coaching Education and Development in the Institute for the Study of Youth Sports (ISYS) at Michigan State University. He is the first author of Chapters 2 and 3. Dr. Lauer has a PhD in exercise and sport science, sport psychology and is the lead consultant for Championship Performance Consulting. He is the Sport Psychology Consultant to USA Hockey's National Team Development Program and consults with athletes, teams and coaches from the youth to professional levels of sport.

Dr. Lauer is a coaching educator for USA Hockey and the Michigan High School Athletic Association, and his parent research has been featured by the National Federation of State High School Associations and the American Sport Education Program. He also assists the USTA in junior player camps and parent workshops and was the lead editor and author of the *USTA Mental Skills and Drills Handbook*.

An AASP Certified Consultant and listed in the United States Olympic Committee Sport Psychology Registry, 2008-2012, Dr. Lauer was named one of the 100 Most Influential Sport Educators in America by the Institute for International Sport.

APPENDIX
Wrestling Match Goal Form

GOAL FORM

——— *PRE-MATCH* ———

What are your two or three performance or process goals for this match (or tournament)?

1

2

3

What are your strategies for achieving those goals?

1

2

3

How will you know if you have achieved your goals?

1

2

3

——— *POST-MATCH* ———

To what degree did you meet goal #1?

Didn't meet goal   Completely met goal

1   2   3   4   5   6   7   8   9   10

To what degree did you meet goal #2?

Didn't meet goal   Completely met goal

1   2   3   4   5   6   7   8   9   10

To what degree did you meet goal #3?

Didn't meet goal   Completely met goal

1   2   3   4   5   6   7   8   9   10

COMPETITIVE REFLECTIONS

Circle your feelings going into and durning the match...

	1	2	3	4	5	6	
No confidence in my physical preparation	1	2	3	4	5	6	Completely confident in my physical preparation
Did not execute strategy or plan at all	1	2	3	4	5	6	Completely executed strategy or plan
Very distracted, not able to block out distractions	1	2	3	4	5	6	Completely focused, blocked our distractions
Did not cope well with pain, factors outside of my control	1	2	3	4	5	6	Coped well with pain, factors outside of my control
Did not have a clear sense of purpose for the match	1	2	3	4	5	6	Had a clear sense of purpose for the match
No determination	1	2	3	4	5	6	Completely determined
Very worried	1	2	3	4	5	6	No worries at all
No physical activation (flat)	1	2	3	4	5	6	Highly physically activated (pumped and positive)
No commitment to push myself	1	2	3	4	5	6	Completely commited to push myself

List at least two things that went well in the match/tournament.

What did not go as well as you would have liked during the match/tournament?

WHAT OTHERS ARE SAYING

"In the *Wrestling Drills For the Mat and the Mind*, Dr. Dennis Johnson has complied drills for every level of wrestling. But he doesn't stop with the physical drills wrestlers are familiar with. He also offers drills for the mind that build a wrestler's mental skills, an important area often overlooked by athletes and coaches alike. This book is an essential tool for all who desire to become the best."

— Bruce R. Baumgartner,
Olympic and World Champion Wrestler

"Intense drilling is critical for success and it is essential to have a variety of drills to maximize intensity daily. Dr. Johnson has created a great resource for coaches at all levels to add new drills to their training program. In addition to skill drills, there are also many unique mental skills exercises designed to develop mental toughness—a critical element for success in our sport."

— Ken Chertow,
US Olympian, 3x NCAA
All-American at Penn State

"Dennis Johnson's *Wrestling Drills for the Mat and the Mind* is an excellent source of information for any coach or athlete looking to expand their wrestling knowledge. It has given me tools I use regularly to keep my practices fresh and my athletes attentive. I encourage all in the wrestling world to use this book to enhance their wrestling experience."

— Marcie VanDusen,
Menlo College Head Women's
Wrestling Coach, US Olympian